BLACKSTONE FRANKS
GUIDE TO
PERKS FROM SHARES

BLACKSTONE FRANKS GUIDE TO PERKS FROM SHARES

KOGAN PAGE

Copyright © Blackstone Franks 1988

All rights reserved. No reproduction, copy or transmission of this publication may be made without written permission.

No paragraph of this publication may be reproduced, copied or transmitted save with written permission or in accordance with the provisions of the Copyright Act 1956 (as amended), or under the terms of any licence permitting limited copying issued by the Copyright Licensing Agency, 7 Ridgmount Street, London WC1E 7AE.

Any person who does any unauthorised act in relation to this publication may be liable to criminal prosecution and civil claims for damages.

First published in Great Britain in 1988 by
Kogan Page Limited, 120 Pentonville Road,
London N1 9JN

British Library Cataloguing in Publication Data

The Blackstone Franks guide to perks from
    shares. — 3rd ed.
 1. Stockholders
 I. Blackstone Franks & Co.
 II. Ramsey, Alan. *Perks from shares*
 332.63'22   HG4661

 ISBN 1-85091-531-8
 ISBN 1-85091-523-7 Pbk

Photoset in North Wales by
Derek Doyle & Associates, Mold, Clwyd.
Printed and bound in Great Britain by
Biddles Ltd, Guildford

Contents

Acknowledgements 6
Introduction 7
Index of Companies 15
Shareholders' Concessions 19
Appendices
1. Trade Names 81
2. Index of Concessions Offered 85
3. Rating of Concessions Offered 91
4. Value of Minimum Consideration 95

Index 103

Acknowledgements

This book has been researched by Patricia H Franks, BA, and Anita Saunders of Blackstone Franks. Robert Leach, ACCA, a Blackstone Franks consultant, was the editor.

> September 1987
> Blackstone Franks & Co
> Chartered Accountants &
>   Investment Managers
> 26-34 Old Street
> London EC1V 9HL

Introduction

Shareholders' concessions, or perks, are gifts, special offers or other benefits which a company offers to its shareholders.

Shares are owned to generate wealth both by receiving dividends regularly (usually twice a year) and by selling them at a profit. Concessions have only a small role to play. The value of the concession may make a share marginally more attractive than it would otherwise be, or, it may increase the share price by encouraging interest in the company and its products or services.

All this, however, is marginal and, with a few exceptions, concessions should be seen as a perk, and not usually considered as a reason for holding a particular share at all. But if you find that your holding is just below the minimum needed for a concession, it may be worth buying a few more shares to qualify.

Many concessions have been lost as the companies have been taken over. The 10 per cent discount on Horizon holidays was lost when the company was bought by Bass. The discounts on double glazing and patio doors offered by London and Midland Industrials were lost when the company was taken over by Williams Holdings.

Other concessions have been lost as the subsidiaries which provided them have been sold. Thus Beechams no longer offer a discount on wine, Thorn-EMI no longer give a discount on electrical appliances, and Rank Organisation no longer give discounts on Wings holidays.

Concessions are not always lost in this way, though. Evered Holdings plc has continued the discount on Weatherseal double glazing previously offered by London and Northern Group.

One area which has particularly suffered is electrical goods. It is known that retailers lobbied strongly against shareholders' discounts and with some effect.

Of those concessions still offered, most are designed to

stimulate the shareholders' interest in the company's products. Many simply take the form of discounts no more generous than would be normal for a typical marketing campaign. Some ferry and holiday companies limit the concession to off-season bookings which does not seem over-generous.

A few concessions are designed to encourage interest in how the company works. Burton's shareholders were given a conducted tour of a new Debenhams store, while shareholders in Fobel International were offered a subsidised trip to the company's new premises in Hong Kong (132 went).

Other concessions are given to encourage shareholders to attend the AGM. You will be given a buffet lunch by Cliffords Dairies, a bottle of drink by Guinness, and a bag of pharmaceutical goods from the Beecham Group.

At the other extreme, a few concessions are so great in value that they provide most, or all, of the reason for buying the shares. The most famous example of this is the concessionary preference share offered by European Ferries, now part of P & O.

These concessions, first introduced in 1959, were particularly generous, offering discounts up to 50 per cent. The number of shareholders grew 60 per cent from 100,000 to 160,000 between 1981 and 1984, mainly due to the concessions. However, when the company decided to give shareholders what was effectively a choice between concessions or voting rights, there were strong objections. Those who wanted concessions did not see why they should be disenfranchised. The share split was effected, but on acceptable terms. When P & O took over European Ferries the holders of these concessionary preference shares were offered similar concessionary shares in P & O. As an inducement the interest rate was increased from 5 per cent to 5½ per cent. The offer was accepted.

Three privately owned railway companies pay no dividends on their shares but provide their shareholders with free tickets on the railways. Here the shares are effectively enthusiasts' contributions. Although the railways are run commercially, profit does not seem to be the prime motive.

Discounted goods range from saucepans (Mellerware) to gold toothpicks (Lonrho). In value they range from a free dry cleaning bag worth £2 (Sketchley) to hundreds of pounds off a new house (Barratts).

Unless otherwise stated, the offers are only available to individual shareholders. Where the company has stipulated this, so have we. Exceptionally, some companies allow corporate shareholders to nominate a user, and this is also expressly stated where appropriate.

Any minimum holding is given, but many offers have no such limit. It is therefore possible to benefit even if you hold only one share. The dealing costs on one share, however, will usually outstrip any other possible benefit of owning shares. It is usually not worth holding less than £500-worth of shares in any one company.

On a strict reading of tax law, it seems that shareholders' concessions can give rise to both an Advance Corporation Tax liability on the part of the company and a potential income tax liability for the shareholder. However, the Inland Revenue say that they have never taxed either the company or the shareholder and have no intention of doing so at present.

Share ownership

There are many types of share now available. The most common is the ordinary share. If you own a company's shares you own part of that company. For example, Trusthouse Forte has one billion shares. If you own 500 Trusthouse Forte shares (enough to qualify you for the concessions) you own 0.00005 per cent of the company.

You do not, however, have the right to tell the company what to do, or even to be informed of all its decisions. You have the right to attend the AGM and ask questions, to vote on issues put forward at the AGM, to receive any dividend which is declared, and to receive a copy of the annual accounts (which are usually part of a book which also contains a report on the company's activities).

The shareholders also appoint the directors and the auditors. But in practice this has usually been sorted out by the directors in advance and it is very rare for shareholders not to accept the directors' recommendations. There are other rights regarding minority interests, access to registers, liquidations and certain types of share issue.

There are also 'A' shares (and sometimes 'B' and 'C' shares as well). These are ordinary shares but with different voting rights – usually none at all. Owning such an 'A' share entitles you to the dividend but not to vote.

Preference shares and debentures represent loans to the company rather than ownership of it. Holders of preference shares and debentures usually receive a fixed rate of interest on their holding. If you have 100 £1 7 per cent preference shares, you will (almost always) receive £7 dividend or interest regardless of how well or how badly the company has done.

Preference shares are usually 'cumulative' and 'non-participating', but do not have to be. 'Cumulative' means that if the company has done so badly that it cannot pay a dividend to the preference shareholders, the dividend owed is added to next year's dividend. If it is non-cumulative, the unpaid dividend is lost. Preference shareholders and debenture holders usually have the right to appoint an administrative receiver if they feel that their interest is being prejudiced.

'Non-participating' means that the holder does not 'participate' in the profits of the company (beyond his fixed interest).

Sometimes such shares or debentures are called 'redeemable' or 'convertible'. 'Redeemable' means that the company can buy them back from you. This may be compulsory or optional; it may be at the discretion of the company or the holder; it may be at a fixed date or not – it depends on the conditions of their issue. 'Convertible' means that you can exchange the preference shares or debentures for ordinary shares. Like redeemable shares, the terms of the conversion depend on the conditions of their issue.

'Stock' is similar to shares, but instead of expressing your holding as a number, it is expressed as an amount. Owning £100-worth of stock in a company with issued stock of £1 million is effectively the same as owning 100 shares in a

INTRODUCTION

company with 1 million shares in issue. In the USA 'common stock' is the equivalent of 'ordinary share'.

For convenience, details of share values are given at the end of each company report. We would stress, though, that the inclusion of a share in this book is not to be taken as a recommendation of it.

Further details of share ownership are given in many comprehensive books now generally available.

Growth in shareholders

Owning shares has become very popular in the last few years. This has been actively encouraged by the present government. There are now an estimated 8.5 million shareholders in the country.

Generous tax incentives have been given, particularly the halving of stamp duty on share transfers and the advent of personal equity plans.

Pressure on the Stock Exchange to end what the government saw as restrictive trade practices led to the 'Big Bang' in October 1986. This abolished fixed commissions and meant that the standard 1.65 per cent commission for low value transactions was replaced with rates as low as 1 per cent. The opportunity was also taken to modernise the share dealing methods using modern computer equipment, and to provide a 24-hour dealing facility under which London, New York and Tokyo each keep their exchanges open for eight hours a day.

Probably the biggest incentive of all has come from the government's programme of privatising state-owned industries. The government has sold shares before – the Labour government sold some BP shares back in 1977 – but the share issues since 1982 have been much larger and had a profound effect on the whole economy.

Amersham International was the first and surprised everyone with its success. The subsequent flotations of British Gas, British Telecom, the Trustee Savings Bank, and the sale of the government's remaining holding in BP are the largest share issues the world has ever seen. All the government's privatisation share issues have gone to an immediate

11

premium, excepting Britoil and BP.

The sudden large increase in the number of shareholders created problems for stockbrokers. These new investors were not wealthy aristocrats with large portfolios worth tens of thousands of pounds; they were ordinary suburban middle-class types with modest portfolios of a few hundred pounds. Many first-time shareholders were more interested in making a quick profit by selling new issue shares soon after purchase (known as 'stagging') than in holding them for years for their capital growth.

Soon after the Big Bang these small investors were wooed by stockbrokers with special offers. Some were known as 'no frills' services. The investor simply rang his broker and gave orders as to what to buy or sell; the stockbroker made no decisions for the investor or gave him any advice. Some stockbroking firms issued membership cards to this new class of investor.

By the summer of 1987 the system had broken down. The stockbrokers who had accepted all this work proved incapable either of processing all the paperwork it generated or of providing even the most basic follow-up service. Paperwork was still outstanding on share transactions completed six months earlier. Small investors found the telephone numbers they were given permanently engaged or just not answered, with the result that shares could have fallen in value by up to 25 per cent before they were able to communicate the instruction to sell. Even then further delays in executing the instructions meant that bargains were often completed at less favourable prices than they should have been.

The Stock Exchange was forced to intervene and introduced two new rules, one of which allowed them to fine firms which failed to process paperwork in time. Improvements were also made in the share certificate registration process.

Curiously, none of this seemed to dampen the enthusiasm for share buying. Over 6 million people registered for priority share applications in BP in October 1987. This left a large market in need of a good service. When deregulation occurred in the USA in 1975, the consequences were similar:

shareholders were first wooed, then ignored, and finally catered for by firms specialising in such a service. It is still too early to say what will happen in the UK, but perhaps a surprising development has been the banks' attitude.

Because of other government pressures on them (such as liberalising the competition from building societies), banks have seized on the opportunity to offer sharebroking facilities to their customers. National Westminster Bank, in particular, has launched a very successful and cost-effective scheme using computer terminals in its larger branches. The scheme is limited to one company's shares at a time, which in practice is always the last big privatisation issue. It is planned to extend both the size and scope of the scheme. The other banks are also pioneering share-dealing services.

Another development is the 'share shop', designed to make buying and selling shares as easy as buying a pair of trousers. Debenhams, in particular, is introducing this facility into its stores.

It seems likely that shareholders in future years will not have to put up with the poor service they suffered in 1987, as specialist stockbrokers, banks and share shops cater for their needs.

The Financial Services Act 1986 will give investors better protection when it becomes fully effective in 1988.

Development of concessions

Concessions have played no significant role in the growth of the number of private shareholders.

Concessions in the form of discount vouchers were offered in British Gas and British Telecom when privatised. Such concessions, however, do not discourage stagging the shares (selling soon after purchase). On the contrary, stagging has become so popular that there is now a 'grey market' where it is possible to sell shares before they have been issued to you.

These concessions attached to the shareholder not the shares, and were therefore lost when the shares were sold. This did not stop the stagging, so the government has moved away from concessions for its big privatisation issues in favour of loyalty bonuses. Under this scheme a shareholder who owns his shares for, say, five years from issue will receive an extra free share for every ten or so held. How effective this will prove has yet to be seen.

A further blow to concessions comes from personal equity plans (PEPs). These allow a person to invest up to £2400 a year free of income tax and capital gains tax. Tax savings which can easily run into hundreds of pounds are more of an inducement to invest than a few cheap saucepans and discounted restaurant meals.

However, they go further in obstructing the use of concessions. It is a rule of authorisation for a PEP that the shareholder must be able to exercise his full rights as a shareholder. But the rules also allow the PEP manager to charge for this. All PEPs so far authorised have made this charge, so the shareholder could easily find that, in practice, he has to pay for his 'free' benefit. Indeed, as he has to pay simply to receive a copy of the annual report, he may not even know that there is a concession available.

In short, most concessions should be seen as a useful little extra. They add fun and interest to share ownership, but their potential still remains largely untapped.

From 1975 to October 1987 share prices increased steadily in the longest ever bull market. On 16 October 1987 the Dow-Jones Index, the US equivalent of the FT Index, fell a record 108.36 points. On 'black Monday', 19 October, the Index fell by a spectacular 508.32 points. As share-dealing is now international these falls were reflected round the world. In the UK, the FT-SE 100 Index fell from 2301.9 to 2052.3 in one day and continued downward in the following weeks. The fall was overdue as share prices were in excess of their underlying values; but it still caught everyone out! However, shares are still a good long-term investment for the individual. Someone who had bought British Gas or British Telecom shares and sold them after the crash would still have shown a good profit, and values in the UK have only fallen to those standing 12 months ago.

Index of companies

Abbey Life Assurance Company Ltd
Abercorn Place School plc
Alexanders Holdings plc
Alexon Group plc
All England Lawn Tennis Ground
Allied-Lyons plc
Ann Street Brewery plc
Asprey plc
Associated British Foods plc
Barclays Unicorn Unit Trusts
Barker and Dobson Group
Barr and Wallace Arnold Trust plc
Barratt Developments plc
Bass plc
Beecham Group plc
Bellway plc
Bentalls plc
Berry Birch and Noble plc
Boots Company plc
Britannia-Arrow Holdings
Britannia Security Group plc
N Brown Group plc
BSG International plc
Burton Group plc
Cattle's (Holdings) plc
Cliffords Dairies plc
Courts (Furnishers) plc
Cramphorn plc
Crown House plc
David & Charles Publishers plc
DFDS (UK) Ltd
Dominion International Group plc
Eldridge Pope & Co Ltd
Emess Lighting plc

PERKS FROM SHARES

European Ferries Group plc
Evered Holdings plc
Ferguson Industrial Holdings plc
Fobel International plc
Fredericks Place Holdings plc
Fuller Smith & Turner plc
Garfunkels Restaurants plc
Gieves Group plc
GRA Group plc
Grand Metropolitan Hotels plc
Greenall Whitley plc
Greene King and Sons plc
Guinness plc
Hawley Group plc
Hillards plc
Isle of Man Steam Packet Seaways
Kalon Group plc
Kennedy Brookes plc
John Kent (Menswear) Ltd
Kwik-Fit (Tyres & Exhausts) Holdings plc
Ladbroke Group plc
Lonrho plc
LWT (Holdings) plc
Manchester and London Investment Trust
Manders (Holdings) plc
Mellerware International plc
Merrydown Wine plc
Moss Bros
Mount Charlotte Investments plc
Norcros plc
Norfolk Capital Group plc
North Norfolk Railway plc
Oriflame International SA
Pacific Sales Organisation
Park Food Group plc
Peninsular and Oriental Steam Navigation Company
Pentos plc
Alfred Preedy plc
Queens Moat Houses plc
Rank Organisation plc

INDEX OF COMPANIES

Ranks Hovis McDougall plc
Romney Hythe & Dymchurch Railway plc
Rover Group plc
Savoy Hotel plc
Scottish and Newcastle Breweries plc
Severn Valley Railway (Holdings) plc
Sharpe & Fisher plc
Sketchley plc
Southampton Isle of Wight and South of England Royal Mail Steam Packet plc
Stakis plc
Stylo plc
Toye & Company plc
Trafalgar House plc
Trusthouse Forte plc
E Upton & Sons plc
Vaux Group plc
Whitbread & Company plc
Yale and Valor plc
Young & Co's Brewery plc

Shareholders' Concessions

Abbey Life Assurance Company Ltd**

Abbey Life House, PO Box 33,
80 Holdenhurst Road, Bournemouth BH8 8AL.　　　0202 292373

Discount on unit trusts

Qualification: One share

Summary of concessions: In 1987 the company made three special offers to its shareholders; each offer was of a 5 per cent discount on the purchase of unit trusts.

In October 1986 the concession was an Investment Bond; in April 1987 it was an Investment Trust; and in October 1987 it was on their Ethical Trust. The company also offered a 5 per cent discount on its Master Trust plan in June and July 1987, and intends to continue making such offers to its shareholders.

The offers are made in conjunction with the issues of the annual report and interim statement.

Share information at 30 September 1987:
　Nominal value: 5p
　Price: 335½p
　Minimum commitment: 335½p
　Yield: 3.3
　Year's high/low: 337½/211p

Abercorn Place School plc***

28 Abercorn Place, London NW8 9XP.　　　01-935 5820

Subsidised and priority education

Qualification: 3500 shares

Summary of concessions: Every tranche of 3500 shares entitles the shareholder to a discount of £120 per term against the school fees. (The current fees are £950 a term for all-day pupils aged 4 to 11, and £575 a term for half-day nursery pupils aged 2½ to 4.) The shareholder nominates the child for whom the concession applies, but only one discount is given for any particular child. The concession attaches to the shares and so passes to a new shareholder.

The school opened in the autumn of 1987. The shares were floated under the BES scheme. Exercising the share concession can result in the loss of some tax relief.

Applications by shareholders for places at the school are given priority over other applications, provided the child meets the educational standards.

Share information at 30 September 1987:
not quoted

Alexanders Holdings plc**

256 West George Street, Glasgow G2 4QY.   041-248 4523

Discount on cars

Qualification: 2000 shares

Summary of concessions: Any shareholder who holds at least 2000 shares is entitled to a discount on a new vehicle bought from the company. The discount is 'around 2 per cent' depending on trade conditions at the time. This discount is in addition to any other discount the shareholder may negotiate.

The company has four branches: in Edinburgh, Greenock, Kirkintilloch and Northampton. All the branches are Ford main dealers.

Share information at 30 September 1987:
Nominal value: 10p
Price: 43½p
Minimum commitment: £870

Yield: 2.2
Year's high/low: 64/14½p

Alexon Group plc**

Alexon House, Kiln Farm, Milton Keynes MK11 3EE.　　0908 565758

Discount on clothes

Qualification: 1000 shares

Summary of concessions: Holders of 1000 or more shares are entitled to a 15 per cent discount on full price Alexon goods at Alexon shops and certain Alexon concessions.

Alexon sell 'women's ready to wear clothing which appeals to fashion conscious customers who want high quality'.

The discount is obtained on presentation of a special card provided on application to the company secretary.

Share information at 30 September 1987:
　Nominal value: 10p
　Price: 433p
　Minimum commitment: £433
　Yield: 1.9
　Year's high/low: 438/111p

All England Lawn Tennis Ground***

Hill House, 1 Little New Street, London EC4A 3TR.　　01-353 8011

Ticket for tennis championship; related benefits

Qualification: £500 of non-interest bearing debenture stock

Summary of concessions: A holder of £500-worth of non-interest bearing debenture stock is entitled to a free ticket for the Centre Court during the Wimbledon tennis championships.

The holders are also entitled to use a special debenture holders' lounge and champagne bar, and may obtain car parking for a small extra fee.

Holders of existing debentures will be given priority for the next series of debenture stock to be issued in 1990.

PERKS FROM SHARES

Share information at 30 September 1987:
not quoted

Allied-Lyons plc*

Allied House, 156 St John Street, London EC1P 1AR.   01-253 9911

Meal vouchers; discount on cruise; discount on liquor; subsidised business planner; discounted holidays

Qualification: One share

Summary of concessions: A book outlining shareholders' perks is sent with the annual accounts. The back of the book contains coupons for the special offers.

The coupons for liquor offer discounts from 25p for a bottle of cider to £1 off a bottle of Courvoisier cognac, Lanson champagne and 12 cans of Castlemaine XXXX. The total value of the vouchers is £15.30. The vouchers are redeemable at Victoria Wine stores. In Scotland they are redeemable at branches of Haddows. These vouchers may only be used by shareholders who are at least 18 years old.

Cases of wine and fortified wine are offered at discounted prices. The discounts range from 19 per cent for sherry (four bottles reduced from £26.92 to £21.85) to 7 per cent for champagne (12 bottles of Harveys Pirrot reduced from £102.35 to £95.22). Any shareholder ordering three or more cases also receives a free bottle of Harvey's of Bristol sherry, worth £2.95.

A bottle of 25-year-old Courvoisier cognac may be purchased for £27.50.

Up to two £2 vouchers, each of which may be for two people, is offered against the £7 fare for a five-hour tour of Loch Lomond on the *Countess Fiona*.

One meal voucher for £3 and two meal vouchers for £1.50 each are provided for part payment of a meal at specified restaurants throughout the country, subject to a few limitations.

A business planner from George Ballantine & Son Ltd may be bought for £40, a 30 per cent discount on the full price of £57.21.

Embassy Hotels offer four £15 vouchers against Embassy Hushaway Breaks. The breaks comprise two nights away including bed, breakfast and evening meal. Leisure activities such as sport, photography and wine-tasting may be taken up. Only one voucher may be used against the price of an adult room per booking.

Share information at 30 September 1987:
Nominal value: 25p
Price: 442p
Minimum commitment: £4.42
Yield: 3.5
Year's high/low: 471/317p

Ann Street Brewery plc*

57 Ann Street, St Helier, Jersey. 9534 31561
Discount on hotel accommodation

Qualification: 100 shares

Summary of concessions: A holder of at least 100 ordinary shares is entitled to a discount of 25 per cent on the standard rate for bed and breakfast at St Pierre Park Hotel, Guernsey.
The discount cannot be used if accommodation is provided as part of a package tour.

Share information at 30 September 1987:
not quoted

Asprey plc**

165-169 New Bond Street, London W1Y 0AR. 01-493 6767
Discount on jewellery, fine arts and antiques

Qualification: 3375 shares

Summary of concessions: Qualifying shareholders are sent a card which entitles them to 15 per cent discount on most purchases in the company's shops in Bond Street and Fenchurch Street in London.

Share information at 30 September 1987:
  Nominal value: 25p
  Price: 310p
  Minimum commitment: £10,462.50
  Yield: 1.8
  Year's high/low: 342/182p
  Quoted on the Unlisted Securities Market

Associated British Foods plc*

Weston Centre, 68 Knightsbridge, London SW1X 7LR.   01-589 6363
Free bag of groceries

Qualification: One share

Summary of concessions: All shareholders who attend the AGM are given a bag of groceries worth a few pounds.

Share information at 30 September 1987:
  Nominal value: 5p
  Price: 343p
  Minimum commitment: £3.43
  Yield: 2.9
  Year's high/low: 416/250p

Barclays Unicorn Unit Trusts**

Juxon House, 94 St Paul's Churchyard, London EC4M 8EH   01-248 9155
Discount on cruises

Qualification: One unit

Summary of concessions: Unitholders in these unit trusts qualify for a discount of between £100 and £250 on a Barclays Unicorn Holiday. The discount is about one sixth of the usual fare.

The holidays are cruises on the *QE2*, *Vistafjord*, and *Cunard Countess*. A choice of 12 holidays was offered for 1987. The package includes free first-class rail travel in Great Britain and free parking at Southampton.

Application is made to the company.

Information at 30 September 1987:
  Price: various
  Minimum commitment: minimal
  Yield: various
  Year's high/low: various

Barker and Dobson Group*

Huntley Mount Road, Bury, Lancashire BL9 6XL.   061-705 2772
Discount on confectionery

Qualification: One share

Summary of concessions: Each June when the annual accounts are sent out, shareholders are invited to purchase high-class chocolates made by Charbonnel et Walker at special prices. These range from £10 to £110. The company declined to say what discount is represented by the offer, but it is believed to be in the range of 10 to 30 per cent on normal retail prices.

Share information at 30 September 1987:
  Nominal value: 10p
  Price: 226p
  Minimum commitment: £2.26
  Yield: 0.6
  Year's high/low: 254/145p

Barr and Wallace Arnold Trust plc*

21 The Calls, Leeds LS2 7ER.   0532 436041
Discounts on holidays, hotels and cars

Qualification: 250 shares

Summary of concessions: Shareholders who own at least 250 shares are entitled to 7½ per cent discount on inclusive holidays, 5 per cent discount on hotels, and 10 per cent discount on new cars sold by the group. The concessions are only available to individual shareholders.
  The holidays are sold through Wallace Arnold Tours Ltd,

PERKS FROM SHARES

Leeds and Wallace Arnold Tours (Devon) Ltd, Paignton. The holiday must be booked through one of the company's offices, not a travel agent.

Discounted hotel accommodation is available from Oswalds Hotel, Torquay.

Vauxhall/Opel cars are sold by WASS (Leeds) Ltd and Trust Motors in Nottingham. Volkswagen and Audi cars are sold by Trust Motors, based in Leeds, Bradford, York and Edinburgh. Ford cars are sold by Trust Motors in Glasgow and Motherwell. The motor vehicles must be bought through one of these dealerships. No discount is given if there is a trade-in.

Share information at 30 September 1987:
Nominal value: 25p 'A' share
Price: 292p
Minimum commitment: £730
Yield: 3.8
Year's high/low: 300/132p

Barratt Developments plc***

Wingrove House, Ponteland Road,
Newcastle upon Tyne NE5 3DP.   091-286 6811

Discount on houses

Qualification: 1000 shares

Summary of concessions: An individual who has held at least 1000 ordinary shares for 12 months is entitled to a discount on a new Barratts House. The discount is £500 per £25,000 or part thereof.

Share information at 30 September 1987:
Nominal value: 10p
Price: 225p ex div
Minimum commitment: £2250
Yield: 5.4
Year's high/low: 252/154p

SHAREHOLDERS' CONCESSIONS

Bass plc**

30 Portland Place, London W1N 3DF. 01-637 5499
Discount on holidays

Qualification: 50 ordinary or preference shares

Summary of concessions: Individual shareholders who have at least 50 ordinary or preference shares are entitled to a 15 per cent discount on accommodation at Crest Hotels and 10 per cent discount on Pontin's Holidays. Each shareholder is sent a numbered Shareholder's Benefit Card.

The company owns 90 Crest Hotels in the UK, Netherlands, Germany, Belgium, Italy and Spain. Shareholders are given a 15 per cent discount on accommodation and food when part of an inclusive package. Otherwise the discount does not apply to food and other hotel services. The discount also cannot be used with any other special offer or discount in operation at the time of the booking.

The company offers a 'Two for the Price of One' scheme whereby a twin or double room for double occupancy may be booked at the normal single rate. Forty hotels also offer 'Welcome Breaks' for two to seven days at a reduced rate. The 15 per cent shareholders' discount applies to these offers also.

Booking is by telephoning or writing either to the company or the hotel direct. The shareholders' special rate must be quoted when booking and the benefit card number quoted. All bookings are subject to availability.

Pontin's Holidays are available at 15 full-board holiday centres, eight self-catering holiday villages, and two chalet and caravan parks. The shareholder is entitled to a 10 per cent discount on the normal tariff price for up to four persons.

Booking is made by telephoning the holiday centre direct. The booking is confirmed with a unique reference number and a form is sent. The full remittance must be paid if booking within 28 days of the holiday.

Share information at 30 September 1987:
Nominal value: 25p
Price: £10

Minimum commitment: £10
Yield: 2.3
Year's high/low: £10½/729p

Beecham Group plc*

Beecham House, Brentford, Middlesex TW8 9BD.   01-560 5151

Free pharmaceutical products

Qualification: One share

Summary of concessions: Shareholders who attend the AGM (in July) are given a small gift, as decided just before the meeting. In 1987 the gift was a bag of the company's pharmaceutical products worth a few pounds.

They have discontinued vouchers for obtaining a discount on wines and spirits.

Share information at 30 September 1987:
Nominal value: 25p
Price: 581p
Minimum commitment: £5.81
Yield: 3.1
Year's high/low: 589/437p

Bellway plc***

Dobson House, Regent Centre, Gosforth,
Newcastle upon Tyne NE3 3LT.   091-285 0121

Discount on houses and kitchen units

Qualification: 1000 shares

Summary of concessions: An individual who has held at least 1000 ordinary shares for 12 months is entitled to a 5 per cent discount on the price of a new house, to a maximum discount of £2500. The shareholder is also entitled to a 10 per cent discount on Nixons kitchen units.

Share information at 30 September 1987:
Nominal value: 25p
Price: 288p

Minimum commitment: £2880
Yield: 3.6
Year's high/low: 322/160p

Bentalls plc*

Wood Street, Kingston upon Thames, Surrey KT1 1TX.   01-546 1001

Discount on department store goods

Qualification: 100 ordinary shares

Summary of concessions: Every shareholder who owns at least 100 ordinary shares is automatically sent six privilege purchase discount vouchers. Each of these entitles the shareholder to a 10 per cent discount on goods purchased at the store. The discount is limited to the range £1 to £10.

The company has six stores: in Kingston, Ealing, Worthing, Bracknell, Tonbridge and Tunbridge Wells.

Share information at 30 September 1987:
   Nominal value: 10p
   Price: 178p ex div
   Minimum commitment: £178
   Yield: 2.0
   Year's high/low: 206/136p

Berry Birch and Noble plc*

22-26 Station Road, West Wickham, Kent BR4 0PS.   01-631 1919

Discount on insurance premiums

Qualification: 500 ordinary shares

Summary of concessions: Individual shareholders who own at least 500 ordinary shares are entitled to a 10 per cent discount on insurance for their main residence and household, provided that the policy is effected through one of the group's companies.

The company trades under the names Berry Birch and Noble and R J Lakin.

Share information at 30 September 1987:
   Nominal value: 10p
   Price: 152p

Minimum commitment: £760
Yield: 3.8
Year's high/low: 152/122p
Quoted on the Unlisted Securities Market

Boots Company plc*

Nottingham NG2 3AA.   0602 506111

Discount on goods

Qualification: 100 shares

Summary of concessions: All shareholders who held at least 100 shares in June 1987 were sent ten £1 vouchers. These vouchers can be used against purchases of at least £5 in the company's stores except for books, medicines and gift vouchers. This scheme repeats the 1986 offer though the company secretary stresses that there is no guarantee that the concession will be continued.

The company operates stores under its own name and Children's World.

Share information at 30 September 1987:
Nominal value: 25p
Price: 306p
Minimum commitment: £306
Yield: 3.6
Year's high/low: 329½/229p

Britannia-Arrow Holdings**

80 Coleman Street, London EC2R 5AD.   01-628 6080

Discount on unit trusts

Qualification: 1000 shares held for a year

Summary of concessions: Any shareholder who has held at least 1000 shares for 12 months is entitled to a 2 per cent discount on the purchase of units in any of the group's unit trusts.

Share information at 30 September 1987:
Nominal value: 25p
Price: 211½

Minimum commitment: £2115
Yield: 3.2
Year's high/low: 212/144p

Britannia Security Group plc*

44 Queen Anne's Gate, London SW1H 9AP. 01-222 2516
Discount on personal alarms

Qualification: One share

Summary of concessions: All shareholders are entitled to a 12.5 per cent discount on intruder alarm systems for home or business premises.

Share information at 30 September 1987:
  Nominal value: 10p
  Price: 244p
  Minimum commitment: £2.44
  Yield: 0.8
  Year's high/low: 249/131p

N Brown Group plc*

53 Dale Street, Manchester M60 6ES. 061-236 8256
Discount on direct mail goods

Qualification: One share

Summary of concessions: Individual shareholders are entitled to a 20 per cent discount on the normal catalogue price of goods advertised in the company's mail order catalogue. The catalogue value of shares so ordered must not exceed 20p per share (the nominal value) held. Thus if a person owns 100 shares, he is limited to £20-worth of goods on which he will be given a £4 discount. There is an overriding maximum of £1000-worth of goods for those who hold 5000 or more shares.

The goods must be for the use of the shareholder or his immediate family. The goods must not be acquired for re-sale.

Shareholders order their goods direct from the company on a special order form.

The company issues catalogues under many names including J D Williams, Ambrose Wilson, Oxendale, Heather Valley, Country Garden, Country Kitchen, New Horizons and Comfortably Yours.

Share information at 30 September 1987:
Nominal value: 20p
Price: 890p
Minimum commitment: £8.90
Yield: 1.2
Year's high/low: 890/408p

BSG International plc**

Burgess House, 1270 Coventry Road,
Yardley, Birmingham B25 8BB.   021-706 6155

Discount on cars, leasing and servicing, and on seat belts and child seats

Qualification: One share

Summary of concessions: Shareholders are entitled to a discount on car purchases, leasing and servicing. The discounts vary according to the franchise and the model involved. Shareholders also receive 50 per cent discount on Britax seat belts and child seats for cars.

The company sells cars through Bristol Street Motors who are dealers as shown below:
Birmingham: Ford, Iveco Ford trucks
Banbury: Peugeot
Bromley: Ford
Cheltenham: Ford
Consett: Vauxhall-Opel, Bedford vans
Huddersfield: Vauxhall-Opel, Bedford vans
Leeds: Austin Rover, Freight Rover
Newcastle: Vauxhall, Bedford vans
Nottingham: Volkswagen, Audi
Sherwood: Citron, Fiat
Shirley: Ford

Southampton: Ford, Iveco Ford trucks
Sunderland: Vauxhall, Bedford vans
Worcester: Ford
The company leases cars through Autolease Ltd, Birmingham.
A shareholder obtains the discount by writing to the group company secretary who arranges for the appropriate group company to contact the shareholder direct.

Share information at 30 September 1987:
   Nominal value: 10p
   Price: 96¾p
   Minimum commitment: 96¾p
   Yield: 2.0
   Year's high/low: 109½/48½p

Burton Group plc**

214 Oxford Street, London W1N 9DF. 01-636 8040
Discount on clothes

Qualification: 300 shares

Summary of concessions: An individual who has held 300 or more ordinary shares for three months and is 18 years or over is entitled to a Burton Group Shareholders Card which gives 12½ per cent discount on merchandise sold by the group.

As this is a credit card, application is made by completing a written form in accordance with the Consumer Credit Act 1974. The use of the card is subject to the usual rules and restrictions applicable to credit cards. It should be remembered that balances uncleared by the due date are subject to a high rate of interest. The latest rate notified is 2.2 per cent per month, equivalent to an APR of 29.8 per cent. This rate, though, is subject to change.

Purchases are made as for other credit cards. The 12½ per cent discount is automatically deducted on the monthly statement. The concession is limited to the first £5000-worth of goods purchased during the company's financial year which runs from 1 September to 31 August.

Discounts are not available in the Rayne store in France

and Delman/Miller store in the USA. It is not available against financial services, foods, fashion alteration, carpet workrooms, kitchen installations, gifts and other tokens, estate agency, opticians' services, catering, fur renovation and storage, soft furnishing workrooms, travel agents, and TV and other rental services.

The scheme is administered by the group's subsidiary, Debenhams Finance Ltd.

Eligible stores in which the card may be used are Burtons, Collier, Jackson, Top Man, Principles for Men, Champion Sport, Peter Robinson, Top Shop, Evans, Dorothy Perkins, Principles, Debenhams, Harvey Nichols, Hamleys, Browns of Chester and Rayne UK. The group has 1400 stores in the UK.

At the 1987 AGM transport was provided for shareholders to look round the new Debenhams store in Oxford Street.

Share information at 30 September 1987:
Nominal value: 50p
Price: 288p
Minimum commitment: £864
Yield: 2.7
Year's high/low: 359/249p

Cattle's (Holdings) plc*

Haltemprice Court, 38 Springfield Way,
Anlaby, Hull HU10 6RR.   0482 564400

Discount on household items, travel

Qualification: One share

Summary of concessions: Shareholders are entitled to a 10 per cent discount on products sold by the retail division, 5 per cent discount on Shopachecks, and special offers and incentives on travel.

The retail division, on whose products the 10 per cent discount is available, comprises:
Rosebys: curtains and household textiles
Ewbanks Mail Order: Furniture, carpets, electrical and other speciality lines
Ewbanks Discount Warehouse: furniture and carpets

Turners Furnishing: furniture, carpets and soft furnishings

Shopachecks can be spent in many high street shops including Burtons, Woolworths, British Home Stores, Stylo etc.

On travel, ABTA rules prevent a concession from being offered, but special offers and incentives may be available by contacting the Travel Executive at either of its companies Travelplan or Parkhill Travel.

Share information at 30 September 1987:
not quoted

Cliffords Dairies plc*

Western Road, Bracknell, Berkshire RG12 1QA.   0344 425741

Free lunch

Qualification: One share

Summary of concessions: Shareholders who attend the AGM are given a free buffet lunch.

Share information at 30 September 1987:
Nominal value: 25p
Price: 556p ex div
Minimum commitment: £5.56
Yield: 2.0
Year's high/low: 558/285p

Courts (Furnishers) plc*

The Grange, 1 Central Road, Morden, Surrey SM4 5RX   01-640 3322

Discount on furniture

Qualification: 100 shares held for at least three months

Summary of concessions: A discount of 10 per cent is allowed on any purchase from the company's furnishing stores and Court's Mammoth Superstores (but not from any franchised departments in them).

Share information at 30 September 1987:
   Nominal value: 25p
   Price: 270p
   Minimum commitment: £270
   Yield: 2.5
   Year's high/low: 298/142p

Cramphorn plc*

Cuton Mill, Chelmsford, Essex CM2 6PD.   0245 466221

Discount on garden supplies and plants

Qualification: 600 shares held for at least one year

Summary of concessions: Shareholders are sent a card which entitles them to a 10 per cent discount at a garden centre or pet and garden shop. The discount is not available for discounted items or in conjunction with their gift tokens. Purchases must be made in cash, not by credit card.

Share information at 30 September 1987:
   not quoted

Crown House plc*

2 Lygon Place, London SW1W 0JT.   01-730 9287

Discount on tableware

Qualification: 250 shares

Summary of concessions: Any individual who holds 250 shares is entitled to a 15 per cent discount on tableware products sold by the group. These include Edinburgh Crystal, Thomas Webb Crystal and Derby Tableware. The products are sold in concessions operated in stores.

Share information at 30 September 1987:
   not quoted

David & Charles Publishers plc*

Brunel House, Newton Abbot, Devon TQ12 4PU. 0626 61121

Discount on books

Qualification: One share

Summary of concessions: The company runs a shareholders' club, membership of which entitles the shareholder to a 25 per cent discount on their books subject to a minimum order value of £15.

The company specialises in non-fiction books on craft, fishing, gardening, health, music, natural history, railways, sailing, sport and travel.

Share information at 30 September 1987:
not quoted

DFDS (UK) Ltd**

Scandinavia House, Parkeston Quay,
Harwich, Essex CO12 4QG. 0255 508122

Discount on ships' fares

Qualification: One share

Summary of concessions: In 1986-87 a discount of 25 per cent was offered on a trip on one of the company's passenger ships. To qualify the shareholder must travel on a Monday, Tuesday, Wednesday or Thursday and must book within eight days of travelling; a return journey may be booked further in advance. The concession is limited to the shareholder and one companion. The discount does not apply to package tours, mini-trips and other trips that are specially reduced.

To qualify in 1986-87, the shares had to be registered by 1 June 1986.

The company's passenger ships sail on these routes:
Copenhagen/Oslo
Esbjerg/Harwich
Esbjerg/Newcastle (summer only)
Copenhagen/Torshavn (summer only)

The journey must be booked through head office, stating at the time that the customer is a shareholder.

DFDS is a Danish company.

Share information at 30 September 1987:
quoted on the Danish stock exchange

Dominion International Group plc*

Dominion House, 49 Parkside, London SW19 5NB.   01-946 5522

Participation in an annual draw for free holiday

Qualification: 500 ordinary shares held for at least 12 months

Summary of concessions: Shareholders who have held at least 500 ordinary 20p shares for the 12 months before the annual draw are allowed to take part in the draw, held in the fourth quarter of the calendar year. Six winners are chosen.

Each winner is entitled to a holiday of his choice for two to anywhere that the company has an operating interest. This includes the USA, Europe and the Far East. The company pays all reasonable costs of travel, accommodation and associated expenses to a maximum of £2000 per shareholder.

For joint shareholders, a nomination for one person in the prescribed form must have been received at least 12 months before the draw.

The company's principal activities are financial services, natural resources and property development.

Share information at 30 September 1987:
Nominal value: 20p
Price: 120p
Minimum commitment: £600
Yield: 6.3
Year's high/low: 137/74p

Eldridge Pope & Co Ltd*

The Dorchester Brewery, Dorchester, Dorset DT1 1QT.   0305 64801

Discount on drink

Qualification: One share

Summary of concessions: Discounts are offered on wines, spirits, cider and beer at Christmas time.
 A buffet lunch is also offered to those who attend the AGM.

Share information at 30 September 1987:
 Nominal value: 25p
 Price: 393p
 Minimum commitment: £3.93
 Yield: 2.5
 Year's high/low: 412/376p

Emess Lighting plc*

PO Box 229, 35 Old Queen Street, London SW1H 9JB.   01-222 5630
Discount on light fittings

Qualification: 100 shares

Summary of concessions: Holders of at least 100 shares are entitled to a 30 per cent discount on light fittings sold in retail outlets.

Share information at 30 September 1987:
 Nominal value: 25p
 Price: 501p
 Minimum commitment: £501
 Yield: 1.7
 Year's high/low: 508/289p

European Ferries Group plc***

Enterprise House, Channel View Road, Dover CT17 9TJ.   0732 368000
Discount on ferry services

Qualification: No concessions for ordinary shareholders.

Discounts on ferry services are granted to 'qualifying shareholders'. Such a shareholder must hold 300 redeemable non-cumulative preference shares of £1 each on 31 December 1986 for travel in 1987. The shares must still be held both when the shareholder books and travels.
 From 1 January 1988 the qualification for the full

concession increases to 600 shares. Shareholders with 300 to 599 shares will be entitled to half the discount only.

On 19 January 1987, European Ferries became a wholly owned subsidiary of Peninsular and Oriental Steam Navigation Company (P & O). At the time of going to press, European Ferries shareholders had voted in favour of exchanging their concessionary shares for similar shares in P & O (see the entry under P & O for details), and the conversion was awaiting legal formalities.

Summary of concessions: Shareholders who held at least 300 redeemable non-cumulative £1 preference shares on 31 December 1986 qualify, under the conditions given below, for these discounts on the normal fare for ferry crossings:

Dover and Felixstowe routes:	50 per cent
Portsmouth routes	40 per cent
Larne-Cairnryan	25 per cent

The ferries sail from Dover to Boulogne, Calais and Zeebrugge; from Felixstowe to Zeebrugge; and from Portsmouth to Cherbourg and Le Havre.

The shareholder must travel personally and take a car, motor caravan or motor cycle with him. The shareholder may also take up to three additional adults; two children count as one adult.

The scheme does not apply to corporate shareholders. For joint shareholdings, the first named shareholder is entitled to the concession.

In addition, shareholders qualify for a 50 per cent discount on the Dover-Ostend route operated by Regie Voor Maritiem Transport (RMT) for car ferry services only. This discount may be withdrawn at the directors' discretion.

All concessions apply only to the standard rates for vehicles and accompanying passengers. They do not apply to special rate fares, foot passengers, towed caravans and trailers, inclusive holidays, or to shipboard goods and services. The company offers discounted fares to senior citizens and Forces personnel as part of its ordinary tariff. Such customers cannot combine this concession with their other discount.

Concessionary bookings must be for return (two-way) journeys, but the return journey may be made by a different route. Concessionary tickets cannot be transferred to another ferry company.

There is no limit to the number of concessionary journeys that may be made in the year, but the shareholding qualification must still be met when the journey is booked and when it is made. No preference is given in booking, so shareholders are advised to book early if they wish to travel at peak times.

Concessionary bookings can only be made on the special shareholders' application form which must be sent to the Concessionary Fare Department at the company's head office (address above). Bookings cannot be made by telephone or personal visit. Payment must be made by a UK cheque, banker's draft or telegraphic transfer. Payment cannot be made by credit card or other method.

Share information at 30 September 1987:
now owned by P & O

Evered Holdings plc*

The Courtyard, Pannells Court,
Guildford, Surrey GU1 4EU.   0483 302020

Discount on double glazing, patio doors etc

Qualification: None mentioned

Summary of concessions: In 1987 the company took over the interests of London and Northern Group and decided to continue the shareholders' perks previously offered. These include a 17½ per cent discount on Weatherseal double glazing, replacement windows, patio doors, residential doors and primary and secondary windows.

The company is looking into the activities of its other subsidiaries to see if further concessions should be offered. Two companies particularly being looked at in this context are Green Brothers (garden furniture) and Tactico (cellular telephones).

Share information at 30 September 1987:
Nominal value: 25p

41

Price: 323p
Minimum commitment: £3.23
Yield: 2.1
Year's high/low: 334/189p

Ferguson Industrial Holdings plc*

Appleby Castle, Cumbria CA16 6XH. 07683 51402

Free visit to Appleby Castle

Qualification: One share

Summary of concessions: Up to four people are admitted free to the Appleby Castle Conservation Centre on production of a copy of the annual report and accounts during normal opening hours.
   Visitors to the castle grounds can see an eleventh century Norman keep and Great Hall. The castle is open to the public during summer.

Share information at 30 September 1987:
   Nominal value: 25p
   Price: 392p
   Minimum commitment: £3.92
   Yield: 3.1
   Year's high/low: 403/268p

Fobel International plc**

Eastgate House, 28-34 Church Street,
Dunstable, Bedfordshire LU5 4RU. 0582 607066

Special offers on products being marketed

Qualification: One share

Summary of concessions: There is no fixed policy on shareholders' perks though it is usual to give shareholders free gifts of products currently being marketed, provided they attend the AGM. The gifts have included a free carton of 13-amp plugs to shareholders who attended the AGM. Special offers have been made on home computers, TV games, cordless telephones and small domestic appliances.

Holders of at least 500 shares were invited to a subsidised trip to Hong Kong to see the company's new factory (132 took up the offer).

Details of current offers are sent with the interim and final accounts.

Share information at 30 September 1987:
  Nominal value: 10p
  Price: 172p
  Minimum commitment: £1.72
  Yield: 0.8
  Year's high/low: 174/58½p

Fredericks Place Holdings plc*

1 Fredericks Place, Old Jewry, London EC2R 8HR.   01-600 3677
Free club membership

Qualification: 10,000 convertible deferred shares or 1200 ordinary shares

Summary of concessions: The holding of sufficient shares entitles the shareholder to free membership of the Country Gentlemen's Association (currently £25 a year, or £23 if paid by direct debit).

Membership of the association carries its own benefits, including a free copy of *Your Money*; special offers on wines, spirits, salmon etc; stockbroking facilities and a wine club.

Share information at 30 September 1987:
  not quoted

Fuller Smith & Turner plc*

Griffin Brewery, Chiswick, London W4 2QB.   01-994 3691
Discount on wine

Qualification: One 'A' share

Summary of concessions: Anyone holding 'A' shares is

entitled to a 5 per cent discount on wine and spirits, including port, sherry, liqueurs and vermouth. Delivery is free for the UK mainland.

Share information at 30 September 1987:
   Nominal value: £1
   Price: 535p
   Minimum commitment: £5.35
   Yield: 1.3
   Year's high/low: 535/335p

Garfunkels Restaurants plc*

122 Victoria Street, London SW1E 5LG.   01-834 0585

Discount on meals

Qualification: One share

Summary of concessions: The company's annual report, sent out in May, contains 15 £1 vouchers. These may be used in part payment for a meal at any of the company's restaurants. Only one voucher may be used per meal.

Share information at 30 September 1987:
   Nominal value: 10p
   Price: 260p
   Minimum commitment: £2.60
   Yield: 0.8
   Year's high/low: 283/158p

Gieves Group plc*

1 Savile Row, London W1X 2JR.   01-434 2001

Discount on menswear

Qualification: 600 shares held for three months

Summary of concessions: Each individual shareholder who holds 600 or more ordinary shares is entitled to a shareholder's card after three months. The card entitles the holder to a 20 per cent discount on menswear goods sold at any branch of Gieves & Hawkes, the company's tailoring division.

   Gieves & Hawkes have branches in Bath, Camberley,

Chester, Deal, Eastbourne, Edinburgh, Harrow, London, Malvern, Plymouth, Portland, Portsmouth and Winchester.

All cards expire on 31 December in the year when issued, but a new card is given to every shareholder who still owns at least 600 shares.

Concessions are not given on the company's gift vouchers or on any goods sold at reduced prices.

The concession is only available to individual shareholders. When shares are held in joint names, the first named holder is entitled to the concession.

Share information at 30 September 1987:
Nominal value: 20p
Price: 253p
Minimum commitment: £1518
Yield: 2.0
Year's high/low: 253/138p

GRA Group plc*

94 Summerstown, London SW17 0BH.   01-946 7741
Free greyhound racing

Qualification: One share

Summary of concessions: Shareholders are given a free admission voucher which allows them and a companion to watch greyhound racing at one of its tracks. The voucher also entitles them to free car parking and to drinks worth £2.50.

Share information at 30 September 1987:
Nominal value: 5p
Price: 150p (last price before share was suspended)
Minimum commitment: £1.50
Yield: 0.8
Year's high/low: 165/70p

Grand Metropolitan Hotels plc*

11-12 Hanover Square, London W1A 1DP.   01-629 7488
Discount on meals, accommodation, wines and spirits, spectacles and contact lenses, and fitness equipment

Qualification: One share

Summary of concessions: Each year the company sends out a special shareholders' booklet which contains discount vouchers and offers to buy goods at special prices.

The booklet sent out in February 1987 gave shareholders a £5 discount on a meal for two at Berni Inns or Barnaby's Carvery; reductions of between £4 and £10 at Berni and Chef and Brewer hotels; special offers on a case of wine, and various beers, spirits and fortified wines; 15 per cent discount on spectacles and contact lenses; a free Grand Metropolitan account card; and discounts on fitness products.

Share information at 30 September 1987:
Nominal value: 50p
Price: 579p
Minimum commitment: £5.79
Yield: 2.4
Year's high/low: 605/439p

Greenall Whitley plc*

Wilderspool Brewery, PO Box No 2, Warrington WA4 6RH.   0925 51234

Discount on hotels

Qualification: One share

Summary of concessions: Holders of either ordinary or 'A' shares are entitled to a shareholders' discount card which entitles the shareholder to a 10 per cent discount on accommodation rates at all De Vere and Greenall Whitley hotels.

Share information at 30 September 1987 (ordinary shares):
Nominal value: 25p
Price: 246p
Minimum commitment: £2.46
Yield: 3.1
Year's high/low: 280½/187p

SHAREHOLDERS' CONCESSIONS

Greene King & Sons plc*

Westgate Brewery, Bury St Edmunds, Suffolk IP33 1QT.   0284 63222
Discount on wine

Qualification: One share

Summary of concessions: Shareholders are entitled to a discount on cases of liquor. In 1987 each case contained a total of nine bottles of fine wines and one each of cognac, sherry and port, and sold for £49.18. Delivery is free.

The company did not say what 'substantial discount' this represented. However, it refers to continuing the 1986 offer which offered discounts of 14 to 18 per cent.

The shareholder must be 18 years old. The price includes delivery for the UK mainland only.

Payment is by completing the form sent with the annual accounts. The form only allows for payment by Visa or Access card.

Share information at 30 September 1987:
　　Nominal value: 25p
　　Price: 431p
　　Minimum commitment: £4.31
　　Yield: 2.1
　　Year's high/low: 431/259p

Guinness plc*

Park Royal Brewery, London NW10 7RR.   01-965 7700
Free drink and glass

Qualification: One share, attending the AGM

Summary of concessions: Shareholders who attend the AGM are given a present. In 1987 this comprised a bottle of Kalibur, a Kalibur glass and a miniature of whisky.

Share information at 30 September 1987:
　　Nominal value: 25p
　　Price: 372p (ex div)
　　Minimum commitment: £3.72
　　Yield: 3.4
　　Year's high/low: 389/264p

47

PERKS FROM SHARES

Hawley Group plc**

5 Hanover Square, London W1R 9HE. 01-629 6252

Discount on showers, double glazing, kitchen units etc

Qualification: 500 shares

Summary of concessions: Holders of at least 500 shares are entitled to a discount of 15 per cent on the company's products from Kitchens Direct, Moben Kitchens, Sharps Bedroom Design, Dolphin Showers and Alpine Double Glazing.
  The shareholder must be on the register when ordering and installation must be at the shareholder's registered address.

Share information at 30 September 1987:
  Nominal value: one cent
  Price: 158p
  Minimum commitment: £790
  Yield: 2.4
  Year's high/low: 174½/109p

Hillards plc**

Spen Lane, Gomersal, Cleckheaton,
West Yorkshire BD19 4PW. 0274 874311

Discount on groceries

Qualification: 200 shares

Summary of concessions: The annual report issued in August gave holders of 200 shares or more five vouchers, each of which gives the shareholder a discount of £3 on purchases of at least £30.

Share information at 30 September 1987:
  not quoted

SHAREHOLDERS' CONCESSIONS

Isle of Man Steam Packet Seaways*

PO Box 5, Douglas, Isle of Man. Administration: 0624 23344;
Reservations: 0624 72468

Half-price on ferry tickets

Qualification: £250 stock

Summary of concessions: Stockholders are entitled to concessionary return tickets. To qualify, stock worth at least £250 must be held on 9 April and on the day of travel. The concessionary ticket gives a 50 per cent discount on the usual fare.

The number of concessionary tickets depends on the value of stock held thus:
£250-£499 stock: one
£500-£999 stock: two
£1000-£1499 stock: three
£1500 stock or more: three, plus a return car ticket

The tickets are for the personal use of the stockholder and are not transferable. Between mid-May and mid-September, the concessions may only be used between Monday and Thursday. The concessionary tickets cannot be used on charter sailings.

Share information at 30 September 1987:
not quoted

Kalon Group plc**

Huddersfield Road, Birstall, Batley,
West Yorkshire WF17 9XA.   0924 477201

Discount on paint, wallpaper and other decorating materials

Qualification: One share

Summary of concessions: Shareholders are issued with a discount card which entitles them to 25 per cent discount off the company's products.

Share information at 30 September 1987:
Nominal value: 15p
Price: 47½p

Minimum commitment: 47½p
Yield: na
Year's high/low: 71/29½p

Kennedy Brookes plc*

Wheeler's House, 25a Lisle Street, London WC2H 7BB.   01-437 9711

Discount on meals

Qualification: 500 shares

Summary of concessions: Individual holders of at least 500 shares receive 20 vouchers which entitle them to discounts of various amounts at the company's restaurants.

Share information at 30 September 1987:
   Nominal value: 10p
   Price: 464p
   Minimum commitment: £2320
   Yield: 0.6
   Year's high/low: 467/225p (the 'high' is adjusted regarding a rights issue)

John Kent (Menswear) Ltd*

26-28 Somerton Road, London NW2 1RY.   01-450 3100

Discount on menswear

Qualification: 500 shares

Summary of concessions: Holders of 500 or more of the company's shares are entitled to a discount card which entitles them to a 10 per cent discount on purchases from the group's retail outlets.
   Shareholders' discount cards are obtained from the company's registrars, W H Stentiford & Co. The card is renewed annually.

Share information at 30 September 1987:
   Nominal value: 5p
   Price: 121p

Minimum commitment: £605
Yield: 2.0
Year's high/low: 150/73p

Kwik-Fit (Tyres & Exhausts) Holdings plc*

17 Corstorphine Road, Murrayfield,
Edinburgh EH12 6DD.   031-337 9200

Discount on motor servicing and parts

Qualification: 100 shares

Summary of concessions: Holders of at least 100 shares are entitled to a 10 per cent discount on one purchase a year at any Kwik-Fit or Stop 'n' Steer centre. The purchase must be for a minimum of £5.

Kwik-Fit centres stock and fit tyres, shock absorbers, batteries and radiators. They also offer engine oil and filter change, computerised wheel balancing and alignment, puncture repairs and menu-priced car servicing.

The Stop 'n' Steer centres specialise in supplying and fitting brakes, clutches, steering and suspension. The group operates through 351 outlets which are open for 363 days a year.

The discount is claimed by sending the full bill with the shareholders' bonus offer form to the company secretary. A refund equivalent of 10 per cent of the bill is then given.

Share information at 30 September 1987:
Nominal value: 10p
Price: 220p
Minimum commitment: £220
Yield: 1.4
Year's high/low: 230/95p

Ladbroke Group plc**

Chancel House, Neasden Lane, London NW10 2XE.   01-459 8031

Discount on hotels, holidays and restaurant meals. Other offers

Qualification: One share (which includes warrants and 8 per cent loan stock)

Summary of concessions: Shareholders are provided with a privilege card which entitles them to 10 per cent discount on hotels, 25 per cent off overseas holidays, 10 per cent off UK holidays and 10 per cent off restaurant meals.

The 10 per cent hotel discount is given against the standard room tariff of all Ladbroke hotels, including all restaurant accounts (drinks as well) at the hotel. The discount also applies to any of the company's pre-booked 'Bright Ideas for Weekends Away' holidays. These include Weekaway Motoring Holidays, Weekend Breaks and Special Interest Weekends, but excludes the rail travel. The company operates 47 hotels in Great Britain and eight in Europe.

The 25 per cent holiday discount applies to the accommodation rates at Club In, Eilat (Israel) and Los Zocos, Lanzarote (Canary Islands). This discount is not available over the Christmas, New Year and Easter periods. The discount applies only to the accommodation; flight arrangements must be made separately.

For UK holidays, there is a 10 per cent discount off the brochure price at any Ladbroke Holidays village or centre. The self-catering villages are at Aviemore, Carmarthen Bay, Great Yarmouth, Isle of Wight, Perranporth, St Ives Bay, Scarborough, Seaton, Teignmouth, Torquay and Weymouth. The 'meal-options centres' are at Caister (Norfolk), Middleton-on-Sea (Sussex) and Torbay.

A 10 per cent discount is given for restaurant meals, including drinks, at Asteys steak restaurants. There are Asteys restaurants in Bonvilston, Bridgend, Cardiff, Castleton, Newport and Port Talbot.

For hotels, holidays and restaurant meals, the shareholder books direct with the appropriate company and presents his privilege card on arrival. The cards run to May and are renewed annually by the company's registrars, the Royal Bank of Scotland.

Other offers are regularly made to shareholders to promote various aspects of the company's wide-ranging activities. In the 1987 accounts, one coupon offered a £25 discount on a

Weekend Break for two, which is in addition to the 10 per cent discount already available. Another coupon allowed shareholders to buy Texas Homecare vouchers at a 15 per cent discount. The company has 150 Texas Homecare superstores which sell over 25,000 products.

Share information at 30 September 1987:
Nominal value: 10p
Price: 453p (ex div)
Minimum commitment: £4.53
Yield: 3.9
Year's high/low: 468/295p (the 'high' has been adjusted to reflect a rights issue)

Lonrho plc**

Cheapside House, 138 Cheapside, London EC2V 6BL.   01-606 9898

Discount on liquor, cars, holidays, clocks etc, bed linen and curtains, and Money Observer *magazine.*

Qualification: 100 shares held continuously from 1 March

Summary of concessions: Shareholders' concessions are revised every year on 1 March. A shareholder who has held at least 100 shares continuously from 1 March receives a book containing vouchers offering discounts at the company's subsidiaries. The list below details the discounts offered in 1987 which may be regarded as typical.

Louis Eschenauer offer a case of 12 bottles of fine wine for £71.

Princess Hotels International offer a 20 per cent discount on accommodation and meals to the shareholder and family travelling with him. They have hotels in Acapulco, Bermuda, the Bahamas and Scottsdale, Arizona.

Whyte & Mackay offer special concessions on their range of whiskies. The range includes Whyte & Mackay Special Scotch Whisky, Whyte & Mackay 12-year-old De-Luxe, Dalmore, Old Fettercain, Tomintoul-Glenlivet, Buchanan, Haig and Crawford's Five Star. A case of 12 bottles, with at least one of each, was available for £99.50.

VAG (United Kingdom) and MAN Commercial Vehicles

offer various concessions on Audi and Volkswagen vehicles.

Brentfords offer a 15 per cent discount on their own range of quilts, blankets, sheets etc. They also offer a 10 per cent discount on Rosebys curtains, Wooltons curtains and Bensons beds sold at Brentfords shops.

SEAT concessionaires offer various discounts on SEAT cars imported from Spain.

Southern Watch & Clock Supplies Ltd offer discounts of between 10 per cent and 25 per cent on clocks, watches, barographs, bracelets, brooches, collarettes, pocket watch chains and gold penknives. All Rolex watches are subject to a 10 per cent discount. And a gold toothpick costs a mere £70 instead of the usual £90.

Dutton-Forshaw offer various concessions on their new and used cars and commercial vehicles. They stock Rolls-Royce, Bentley, Jaguar, Daimler, Austin Rover, Vauxhall-Opel, Talbot, Audi Volkswagen and Honda. They also offer shareholders £25 off the manufacturer's recommended major service charge, whatever the make of car.

Metropole Hotels offer a discount on their Short Break holidays. They have hotels in London, Birmingham, Brighton, Blackpool and Mauritius.

Money Observer invites shareholders to a year's subscription for £16, a 13.5 per cent discount on the usual subscription of £18.50. Subscribers are also given a free copy of *Ernie's Missing Millions* which lists all 63,000 unclaimed premium bond prizes.

Share information at 30 September 1987:
Nominal value: 25p
Price: 334½p
Minimum commitment: £334.50
Yield: 4.6
Year's high/low: 334½/223p

SHAREHOLDERS' CONCESSIONS

LWT (Holdings) plc*

South Bank, Television Centre, Kent House,
Upper Ground, London SE1 9LT.   01-261 3434

Discount on holidays

Qualification: 100 shares

Summary of concessions: Holders of at least 100 shares are entitled to a discount on a holiday run by its subsidiary Page and Moy Ltd. The discount is 10 per cent off holidays operated by Page & Moy, and 5 per cent off holidays operated by another ABTA operator and booked through Page & Moy.

The concession applies to the shareholder and his or her family and friends travelling on the same holiday.

Share information at 30 September 1987:
  Nominal value: 25p
  Price: 1008p
  Minimum commitment: £1008
  Yield: 2.5
  Year's high/low: 1010/440p

Manchester and London Investment Trust*

Charlotte House, 10 Charlotte Street,
Manchester M1 4FL.   061-228 2511

Discount, and participation in an annual draw

Qualification: No minimum holding mentioned

Summary of concessions: The company declined to provide proper details, but we understand that they give shareholders vouchers for a 25 per cent discount, and have a draw each year at the AGM.

Share information at 30 September 1987:
  not quoted

Manders (Holdings) plc**

PO Box 186, Old Heath Road, Wolverhampton WV1 2QT.   0902 53122

Discount on paint, brushes and wall coverings

Qualification: One share held by private investor

Summary of concessions: Up to 20 per cent discount on paint, up to 25 per cent discount on brushes, and up to 30 per cent discount on wall coverings from the company's own branches and from some nationwide distributors. These include Manders Paints Ltd, McNeill & Co (Decorations) Ltd and MGB Tiles Ltd. The discount is claimed by presenting a Trade Cash Card which is issued to all private individuals as soon as possible after they become shareholders.

Share information at 30 September 1987:
  Nominal value: 25p
  Price: 385p (ex div)
  Minimum commitment: £3.85
  Yield: 3.6
  Year's high/low: 413/324p

Mellerware International plc*

Middlemore Lane West, Redhouse Industrial Estate,
Aldridge, Walsall, West Midlands WS9 8EA.   0922 56113

Discount on cookware and domestic appliances

Qualification: 250 shares

Summary of concessions: A holder of at least 250 shares is entitled to a 12½ per cent discount on the company's products.
  The shareholder buys the product at the full price and sends the receipt to the head office which refunds the discount. There is a limit of £250 worth of goods per year, but there is no minimum purchase amount.

Share information at 30 September 1987:
  Nominal value: 10p
  Price: 113p

Minimum commitment: £282.50
Yield: 1.3
Year's high/low: 130/67p

Merrydown Wine plc**

Horam Manor, Horam, Heathfield, East Sussex TN21 0JA.   04353 2254
Discount on cider and wine
Qualification: 1000 shares

Summary of concessions: Holders of 1000 shares or more are entitled to buy cases of cider and wine from the company at a discounted price. The shareholder must be 18 years old.

A case of cider, for example, costs a shareholder £16 against the retail price of £19.56. Delivery in the UK is free.

Share information at 30 September 1987:
Nominal value: 25p
Price: 432 (ex scrip issue)
Minimum commitment: £4320
Yield: 1.7
Year's high/low: 432/370p
Quoted on the Unlisted Securities Market

Moss Bros*

21-26 Bedford Street, London WC2E 9EQ.   01-240 4567
Discount on clothes, hire of clothes and sports goods
Qualification: 250 shares

Summary of concessions: Shareholders are automatically sent a plastic discount card when their holding reaches 250 shares. On request a second card is sent for use by the shareholder's husband or wife.

The card entitles its holder to a 10% discount on clothes (including shoes), the hire of clothes, and sporting goods.

It cannot be used to buy clothes in a sale.

Share information at 30 September 1987:
Nominal value: 20p
Price: £12-3/16 (ex div)

Minimum commitment: £3046.88
Yield: 0.7
Year's high/low: £12¼/580p

Mount Charlotte Investments plc*

2 The Calls, Leeds LS2 7JU.   0532 439111
Discount on hotel accommodation

Qualification: 1000 shares

Summary of concessions: Any individual who holds 1000 ordinary shares on 1 March is entitled to discounts on accommodation at the company's hotels. The discounts are announced in April when the annual accounts are published. The discounts are usually in the order of 10 to 15 per cent.

As well as running hotels under the name of Mount Charlotte, the company also owns the Kings Mead group, London Park Hotels, Hospitality Inns, and (in Scotland) Skean Dhu.

Share information at 30 September 1987:
Nominal value: 10p
Price: 155½p
Minimum commitment: £1555
Yield: 1.4
Year's high/low: 164½/94p

Norcros plc*

Spencers Wood, Reading, Berkshire RG7 1NJ.   0734 884567
Discount on meals and accommodation

Qualification: One share

Summary of concessions: Shareholders are issued with a discount card which entitles them to a 10 per cent discount on UBM building supplies and home improvement shops run by the company.

Share information at 30 September 1987:
Nominal value: 25p
Price: 433p

Minimum commitment: £4.33
Yield: 4.4
Year's high/low: 450/246p

Norfolk Capital Group plc*

8 Cromwell Place, London SW7 2JN.   01-581 0601

Discount on hotel accommodation

Qualification: One share

Summary of concessions: Vouchers are sent out to shareholders with the annual report in May. These vouchers give shareholders 20 per cent discount on accommodation in their hotels; 15 per cent discount on meals there; and 10 per cent discount on 'Great Stay' weekends.
  The group owns these hotels:
  Angel Hotel, Chippenham
  Angel Hotel, Glamorgan
  Billersley Hotel, Stratford
  Brigands House Hotel, Stanstead Abbott
  Caledonian Hotel, Edinburgh
  Eastwell Manor Hotel, Ashford
  The Elms Hotel, Worcester
  Norfolk Hotel, London
  North British Hotel, Edinburgh
  Oakleigh Court Hotel, Windsor
  Old Swan Hotel, Harrogate
  Royal Clarence Hotel, Exeter
  Royal Court Hotel, London
  Royal Crescent Hotel, Bath

Share information at 30 September 1987:
  Nominal value: 5p
  Price: 41½p
  Minimum commitment: 41½p
  Yield: 1.2
  Year's high/low: 55½/26½p

PERKS FROM SHARES

North Norfolk Railway plc***

Sheringham Station, Sheringham, Norfolk NR26 8RA.   0263 822045

Free travel on railway

Qualification: 20 shares

Summary of concessions: Shareholders are entitled to free travel on the railway according to the number of shares held.

Holders of 20 shares are given an ordinary pass which entitles them to two second-class return journeys per year (but see below). Holders of 50 shares are entitled to four free journeys a year. Holders of 100 shares are entitled to four free second-class journeys with one guest. Holders of 250 shares are given a gold pass for four free journeys for the shareholder and his family. Holders of 500 shares are given a VIP pass for a free reserved compartment and travel for himself and five guests four times a year. Holders of 5000 or more shares are given a 'statesman' pass entitling the shareholder to the free charter of one train once a year for up to 200 guests. Seven days' notice is requested from holders of 250 or more shares who wish to take advantage of the concessions.

In August 1987 the company made an equity issue of 140,000 ordinary £1 shares at par to fund the building of a new station at Holt. The concession for holders of 20 shares does not apply to these new shares.

The railway runs for 5½ miles between Sheringham and Holt. Much of the journey is within sight of the sea; the area has been designated as one of outstanding beauty. The company uses mainly steam engines and operates at weekends and in holidays. It is largely staffed by volunteers.

The company is profitable but does not pay dividends.

Share information at 30 September 1987:
not quoted

Oriflame International SA*

Goldsmiths Group plc, Goldsmiths House,
Elland Road, Braunstone, Leicester LE13 1TT.   0533 871461

60

SHAREHOLDERS' CONCESSIONS

Discount on jewellery

Qualification: 250 shares

Summary of concessions: In 1987 Oriflame purchased the Goldsmiths group and continued the shareholders' concessions previously offered by Goldsmiths.
 This concession is 15 per cent on all jewellery and watches sold at any of Goldsmiths' 112 shops in the UK. The concession does not apply to sale items and special offers.

Share information at 30 September 1987:
 Nominal value: no par value
 Price: 305p (ex div)
 Minimum commitment: £762.50
 Yield: na
 Year's high/low: 330/205p

Pacific Sales Organisation*

Arnak House, Mary Street, Manchester M3 1EA.   061-832 4986

Nothing

Qualifications: One share; attendance at AGM

Summary of concessions: Shareholders who attend the AGM have been presented with a gift of an item promoted by the company. In 1986 it was a calculator billfold. However, in 1987 no gift was made and a company spokesman doubted if the practice would be resumed in 1988.

Share information at 30 September 1987:
 Nominal value: 10p
 Price: 375p
 Minimum commitment: £3.75
 Yield: 0.6
 Year's high/low: 401/45p

Park Food Group plc*

Valley Road, Birkenhead, Merseyside L41 7ED.　　　051-653 0566
Discount on Christmas hampers

Qualification: One share

Summary of concessions: All shareholders are entitled to a 20 per cent discount on their Christmas hampers.

Share information at 30 September 1987:
　Nominal value: 10p
　Price: 293p
　Minimum commitment: £2.93
　Yield: 2.2
　Year's high/low: 308/170p

Peninsular and Oriental Steam Navigation Company*

79 Pall Mall, London SW1Y 5EJ.　　　01-930 4343
Discount on travel by ship

Qualification: £200 deferred stock or £500 preferred stock

Summary of concessions: Holders of sufficient shares are entitled to a 30 per cent discount on the group's ferry sailings between Aberdeen and Lerwick (Shetland) and Scrabster and Stromness (Orkney). The concession is limited to two round trips a year and does not apply in July and August. A discretionary offer on other cruises has been discontinued.

　On 19 January 1987, P & O became the ultimate holding company of European Ferries (see **European Ferries Group plc,** page 39) and pledged to maintain the concessions offered by those shareholders. Former holders of concessionary 5 per cent preference shares in European Ferries have been invited to exchange them for 5.5 per cent redeemable non-cumulative preference shares in P & O. The European Ferries' concession which attaches to this class as a *legal* right will be maintained by P & O. These arrangements were approved by shareholders on 28 and 29 September 1987 and took effect on 29 October 1987 after the necessary legal formalities had been completed.

Information at 30 September 1987 (£1 deferred stock):
Nominal value: £1
Price: 738p (ex div)
Minimum commitment: £1476
Yield: 3.5
Year's high/low: 776/523p

Information at 30 September 1987 ($6\frac{3}{4}$ per cent preferred stock):
Price: 140p
Minimum commitment: £700
Yield: 6.6
Year's high/low: $149\frac{1}{2}/110\frac{1}{2}$p

Pentos plc*

New Bond Street House, 1-5 New Bond Street,
London W1Y 0SB.   01-499 3484

Discount on books and paintings

Qualification: 500 shares

Summary of concessions: Individual shareholders who hold at least 500 Pentos shares are entitled to a card which gives them 10 per cent discount on purchases in the bookshops and galleries run by the company and its subsidiaries.
   The group owns these bookshops:
Dillons Bookshop; Canterbury, London, Oxford
Hodges Figgis; Dublin
Hooks Books; Bromley, Crawley
Hudsons Bookshops; Birmingham, Croydon, Derby,
    Harrogate, Leicester, Liverpool, London,
    Loughborough, Newcastle upon Tyne, Nottingham,
    Sheffield, Wolverhampton
Hudsons Wessex Bookshop; Chichester
Weatherheads Bookshop; Aylesbury
   They own Athena Bookshops which has branches in Bournemouth, Canterbury, Gateshead, Kings Lynn, London, Maidstone and Southampton.
   They also own Athena Galleries.
   All purchases must be made in cash.

Share information at 30 September 1987:
  Nominal value: 10p
  Price: 177p
  Minimum commitment: £885
  Yield: 0.7
  Year's high/low: 184/85p

Alfred Preedy plc**

Burnt Tree House, Burnt Street, Tipton,
West Midlands DT4 7UG.   021-557 3998

Discounts on domestic goods

Qualification: 250 shares

Summary of concessions: A shareholder who owns at least 250 shares is entitled to a 10 per cent discount on all purchases exceeding £3 made at the group's stores. This includes books, records, tableware, sports equipment, confectionery, cards and toys.

The concession may not be used to obtain a discount on cigarettes, newspapers or magazines.

Share information at 30 September 1987:
  Nominal value: 25p
  Price: 169p
  Minimum commitment: £422.50
  Yield: 3.4
  Year's high/low: 202/121p

Queens Moat Houses plc*

Queens Moat House, St Edwards Way,
Romford, Essex. RM1 4DD.   0708 25814

Discount on meals

Qualification: One share

Summary of concessions: Shareholders are sent three vouchers with the annual report in April or May. Two are worth £5 each and may be used to pay for food and drinks at their hotels; the other is worth £17 and may be used towards the cost of a Town and Country Classics Weekend Break. (The 1986 figures were £4 and £15 respectively.)

The group has 62 hotels in the UK and 18 in Netherlands, Belgium and Germany.

Share information at 30 September 1987:
  Nominal value: 5p
  Price: 108½p
  Minimum commitment: £1.09
  Yield: 2.3
  Year's high/low: 108½/60½p

Rank Organisation plc*

6 Connaught Place, London W2 2EZ.   01-629 7454
Discount on holidays and hotels

Qualification: Either 500 shares held for at least six months, or any number of shares held for five years

Summary of concessions: A shareholder qualifies for a 10 per cent discount on the company's holidays and hotel accommodation if he meets one of the qualification conditions by the date of departure or when he checks in.

Eligible holidays are those provided by Butlin's, Haven Holidays and Blue Line Cruisers. The concession is not available for OSL Travel Plus Club. The discount does not extend to holiday insurance, ski passes, flight supplements, surcharges or other taxes. The concession may be used in conjunction with a Butlin's Guest Offer, but not with other discounted offers. Holidays by Wings were included within the scheme until the business was disposed of in 1987.

The shareholder must participate in the concessionary holiday. There is a limit of £5000 on the cost of the holiday discounted. No priority is given to shareholders in booking.

The concession for hotel accommodation applies to Royal Lancaster, Royal Garden, Gloucester, White House and Athenaeum Hotels in London, and to the Unicorn Hotel in Bristol. The 10 per cent discount applies to the normal published tariff.

Bookings are made directly with the company concerned, not through a travel agent. Immediately after making the reservation, the booking form must be marked 'shareholder 10 per cent discount' and sent to the company.

Share information at 30 September 1987:
  Nominal value: 25p
  Price: 704p
  Minimum commitment: £3520
  Yield: 3.5
  Year's high/low: 826/520p

Ranks Hovis McDougall plc*

RHM Centre, PO Box 178, Alma Road, Windsor,
Berkshire SL4 3ST.   0753 857123

Free groceries

Qualification: One share; attendance at the AGM

Summary of concessions: All shareholders who attend the AGM are given a carrier bag of groceries with a retail value of between £5 and £7.

Share information at 30 September 1987:
  Nominal value: 25p
  Price: 357p
  Minimum commitment: £3.57
  Yield: 2.5
  Year's high/low: 357/278p

Romney Hythe & Dymchurch Railway plc**

New Romney Station, New Romney, Kent TN28 8PL.   0679 63256

Discount on railway journey

Qualification: 100 shares

Summary of concessions: A holder of between 100 and 499 shares is entitled to a pass giving the holder free travel on the railway.
  A holder of between 500 and 4999 shares is entitled to a

silver medallion pass which entitles him and his family to free travel. A holder of 5000 or more shares is entitled to a gold medallion pass which entitles the shareholder and his family and friends to free travel and allows him to hire a train free once a year.

The railway runs for 14 miles between Hythe and Dungeness. The current fare for the journey is £5.10. The company is profitable but is not yet in a position to pay dividends on its shares.

Share information at 30 September 1987:
   not quoted

Rover Group plc**

7-10 Hobart Place, London SW1W 0HH.   01-235 4311

Discount on cars

Qualification: 1000 ordinary shares held for six months

Summary of concessions: £100 off new vehicles in the Austin Rover and Land Rover ranges. The scheme is called SHARDIS.

The car must be purchased from a distributor or main dealer, but not a retail dealer. The shares must have been held continuously for six months before applying under the scheme.

The discount of £100 is additional to any other discount or terms which the shareholder may negotiate with the distributor or main dealer.

To claim the discount, the shareholder must write to the head office for a form of authorisation. This form remains valid for three months.

Share information at 30 September 1987:
   Nominal value: 50p
   Price: 88p
   Minimum commitment: £500

Yield: na
Year's high/low: 103/36p

Savoy Hotel plc*

1 Savoy Hill, London WC2R 0BP.　　　　　　　　01-836 1533
Discount on hotel accommodation

Qualification: One share

Summary of concessions: 10 per cent discount on one or more night's stay at either the Savoy Hotel or the Lygon Arms.

For both hotels the discount applies to the shareholder's total hotel expenditure, but is restricted to certain times. In 1987 discounts at the Savoy applied to weekends from April to August and to weekdays from 13 July to 28 August. At the Lygon Arms, the discount applied from April to October but was not available on Fridays and Saturdays. Concessions for 1988 and later years are likely to be on a similar basis.

Settlement must be by cash or cheque, not credit card.

Share information at 30 September 1987:
Nominal value: 10p
Price: 658p
Minimum commitment: £6.58
Yield: 0.8
Year's high/low: 658/376p

Scottish and Newcastle Breweries plc*

Abbey Brewery, Holyrood Road, Edinburgh EH8 8YS.　　031-556 2591
Discount on accommodation, meals, wines and spirits

Qualification: One share

Summary of concessions: Ordinary shareholders are provided with an accommodation voucher worth £20 and two meal vouchers each worth £5. These could be used in the company's Thistle hotels.

Shareholders must be on the shareholder's register at the end of July.

In 1987 the company also offered a discount on two cases of wines and spirits.

Share information at 30 September 1987:
  Nominal value: 20p
  Price: 261p
  Minimum commitment: £2.61
  Yield: 4.2
  Year's high/low: 268/195½p

Severn Valley Railway (Holdings) plc***

The Railway Station, Bewdley, Worcestershire DY12 1BG.   0299 403816
Free travel on railway

Qualification: 25 shares

Summary of concessions: Free travel is offered on the company's railway according to the size of the shareholding.

Holders of between 25 and 99 shares are entitled to three third-class adult return tickets between Bridgnorth and Southern operational terminus. Holders of between 100 and 499 shares are entitled to four such tickets. Holders of between 500 and 999 shares are entitled to four first-class tickets for the same journey. Holders of 1000 or more shares are given a gold pass which entitles the shareholder and up to four family members to unlimited travel on the railway.

The company runs steam trains between Bridgnorth and Kidderminster. It provides quality meals on the trains and other attractions.

The company is profitable but does not pay dividends on its shares.

Share information at 30 September 1987:
  not quoted

Sharpe & Fisher plc*

Gloucester Road, Cheltenham GL51 8PT.   0242 521477
Discount on building materials and garden centre goods

Qualification: One share

Summary of concessions: All shareholders are given a discount voucher valid to the end of the calendar year. The voucher entitles the shareholder to a 10 per cent discount on the company's goods. The shareholder is restricted to one purchase in the year but there is no limit on the number of items purchased or on their value.

The company operates Sharpe & Fisher building supply depots in Bicester, Cardiff, Cheltenham, Haverfordwest, Hereford and Llanelli. It operates Sandfords DIY and garden centres in Abingdon, Cheltenham, Christchurch, Droitwich, Gloucester, Hereford, High Wycombe, Kidderminster, Newbury, Poole, Redditch, Swindon and Weston-super-Mare.

Share information at 30 September 1987:
  Nominal value: 25p
  Price: 243p
  Minimum commitment: £2.43
  Yield: 1.7
  Year's high/low: 250/134p

Sketchley plc**

PO Box 7, Hinckley, Leicestershire LE10 2NE.　　　　　　0455 38133

Discount on dry cleaning and pronto bag

Qualification: 300 shares (discount); One share (pronto bag)

Summary of concessions: An individual holder of 300 or more ordinary or preference shares is entitled to a shareholder discount card which entitles him to 25 per cent discount on the normal list price charged by the company for dry cleaning.

The card may only be used by the individual shareholder and one nominated member of his or her family. The card may not be used for dry cleaning of items used in the shareholder's business. The cards expire on 31 October and are renewed automatically. The discount is not given with any concession or offer and may not apply to all services offered by the company. The card may be used at all branches of Sketchley Cleaners but not at Sketchley agents or Sketchley Associated Cleaners shops.

In addition all shareholders, regardless of the number of shares held, are given a pronto bag. This is a tagged bag in which dry cleaning is put for a quick and more efficient service. The bags normally cost £2 each.

Share information at 30 September 1987:
  Nominal value: 25p
  Price: 497p
  Minimum commitment: £1491
  Yield: 5.4
  Year's high/low: 569/276p

Southampton Isle of Wight and South of England Royal Mail Steam Packet plc***

12 Bugle Street, Southampton SO9 4LJ.   0703 333042

Discount on ferry and hydrofoil service

Qualification: 2400 shares

Summary of concessions: Holders of at least 2400 ordinary shares of the company are entitled to a free pass which gives them free travel on the company's ferry service between Southampton and Cowes, and a 50 per cent discount on the standard single fare for the hydrofoil service.

The concession is limited to the individual shareholder and does not apply to motor vehicles.

Share information at 30 September 1987:
  Nominal value: 50p
  Price: 665p
  Minimum commitment: £15,960
  Yield: 4.1
  Year's high/low: 675/300p

PERKS FROM SHARES

Stakis plc**

244 Buchanan Street, Glasgow G1 2NB.   041-332 9711

Discount on hotel, meals and holidays

Qualification: 300 shares

Summary of concessions: All holders of at least 300 shares receive discount vouchers with the annual report in January.

This entitles the shareholder to £6 off a meal for two at one of their hotels or steak houses; a 20 per cent discount on a Stakis holiday; and £25 off the cost of a holiday for two at Stakis Resort Hotel Paraiso.

Share information at 30 September 1987:
   Nominal value: 10p
   Price: 122p
   Minimum commitment: £366
   Yield: 1.6
   Year's high/low: 139/78½p

Stylo plc**

Stylo House, Harrogate Road, Apperley Bridge, Bradford, West Yorkshire BD10 0NW.   0274 617761

Discount on shoes and sportswear

Qualification: One share

Summary of concessions: Shareholders are given two discount vouchers, each of which entitles them to a 20 per cent discount on shoes or sportswear goods sold through the company's Stylo or Barratts shops. They have 235 shops in the UK.

The vouchers may not be used in concessions run by the company.

Share information at 30 September 1987:
   Nominal value: 25p
   Price: 336p
   Minimum commitment: £3.36

Yield: 2.0
Year's high/low: 347/226p

Toye & Company plc*

19-21 Great Queen Street, London WC2B 5BE.　　　01-242 0471

Discount on jewellery, regalia, badges, trophies etc

Qualification: 250 shares

Summary of concessions: An individual shareholder who has at least 250 shares is entitled to a numbered 'special purchase card' which gives him 15 per cent discount on all items sold at the company's retail shops or ordered by post from its head office.

The company has shops in London, Edinburgh, Glasgow and Manchester. They specialise in civil and military regalia including badges and mayoral chains; masonic regalia and equipment; Rotary badges; T-shirts and sweat shirts and other leisure wear suitably embroidered or emblazoned; cufflinks, key fobs, badges and silk screened products; and long service awards, medals, proof coins and presentation gavels and blocks.

Share information at 30 September 1987:
　　Nominal value: 25p
　　Price: 230p
　　Minimum commitment: £575
　　Yield: 3.0
　　Year's high/low: 235/126p

Trafalgar House plc*

1 Berkeley Street, London W1X 6NN.　　　01-499 9020

Discount on travel and hotels

Qualification: 250 ordinary shares

Summary of concessions: Holders of at least 250 ordinary shares are offered a 15 per cent discount on most Cunard holidays, 10 per cent discount on the Sagafjord World

Cruise, and 15 per cent discount on hotel accommodation. Institutional and corporate shareholders may nominate one person to enjoy the concessions.

Cunard offer a 15 per cent discount off the published tariffs for most voyages and cruises aboard its seven ships, including the *QE2*. They also offer a 10 per cent discount on the Sagafjord World Cruise and on package holidays incorporating flights on Concorde.

A discount of 15 per cent is offered on accommodation at all Cunard hotels, the Ritz and Stafford Hotels in London, the Cunard Paradise Beach Hotel in Barbados and the Cunard Hotel La Toc in St Lucia.

These discounts cannot be combined with any other promotional tariff.

In addition, shareholders may be able to obtain a discount on either the outright purchase or a quarter timeshare in property in Rocha Brava, the Algarve, Portugal. The discounts were 2½ per cent and 5 per cent respectively until the scheme officially closed on 30 September 1987, but late offers may be accepted at negotiated discounts.

Share information at 30 September 1987:
  Nominal value: 20p
  Price: 398p
  Minimum commitment: £995
  Yield: 4.5
  Year's high/low: 441/274p

Trusthouse Forte plc**

166 High Holborn, London WC1V 6TT.   01-836 7744

Discount on hotel and restaurant bills, sports equipment and wine

Qualification: Either 500 shares, or any number of shares held from 31 October 1985.

Summary of concessions: Shareholders who either hold 500 shares or who were on the share register before 1 November 1985 may purchase Group Leisure Cheques at a discount of 10 per cent to a maximum face value of £2000 for a fixed period. (The 1987 period was 1 April to 31 October.) The cheques have face values of £1, £5, £10 and £50.

The cheques may be used in settlement of bills at hotels and restaurants owned by the company. These include Anchor hotels and Little Chef restaurants as well as Trusthouse Forte hotels. Ring & Brymer accept the cheques for outdoor catering at major sporting events.

They can also be used to obtain a discount on sports equipment from Lillywhites and wine from the Wine Growers Association.

The cheques are obtained by sending a completed form to the company's head office.

Share information at 30 September 1987:
Nominal value: 25p
Price: 271p
Minimum commitment: £1355
Yield: 3.0
Year's high/low: 280½/179p

E Upton & Sons plc*

175-187 Linthorpe Road, Middlesbrough,
Cleveland TS1 4AJ.   0642 244291

Discount on goods sold in department stores

Qualification: 250 ordinary shares

Summary of concessions: 15 per cent discount on goods sold in stores with these exceptions:

10 per cent discount on 'low-margin' goods, which include large electrical items and carpets with free fitting.

No discount is offered on goods substantially reduced in sales, or on goods with free gifts or subject to special offers.

Uptons operates stores under its own name, and also owns McKenna & Brown which sells audio, TV and photographic equipment.

Share information at 30 September 1987:
Nominal value: 25p
Price: 155 (ex div)
Minimum commitment: £387.50

75

Yield: na
Year's high/low: 155/111½

Vaux Group plc*

The Brewery, Sunderland SR1 3AN.   091-514 2488

Discount on accommodation, meals, wines and spirits; free lunch

Qualification: One share

Summary of concessions: All individual shareholders are entitled to a shareholders' discount scheme card. This entitles them to a package of benefits which varies each year.

For 1987 the concessions were a 10 per cent discount on accommodation, restaurant meals and leisure club membership; a sheet of vouchers which provide further discounts on certain mini-holidays; and discounted wine offers from their subsidiary company James Bell & Co.

The company runs Swallow Hotels who own 34 hotels in Great Britain from which the 10 per cent discount on accommodation and meals may be taken. The extra discounts on mini holidays were given by three vouchers, one for £15 and two each for £10.

They also own 30 pubs in north-east England and four Vaux Free Houses in London at which 10 per cent discount is given on meals. The pubs are run by Vaux Breweries Ltd and S H Ward & Co Ltd.

Shareholders who attend the AGM are given a free lunch.

Share information at 30 September 1987:
 Nominal value: 25p
 Price: 569p
 Minimum commitment: £5.69
 Yield: 3.4
 Year's high/low: 579/463p

SHAREHOLDERS' CONCESSIONS

Whitbread & Company plc*

Brewery, Chiswell Street, London EC1Y 4SD. 01-606 4455

Discount on accommodation, sporting events, free wine, savings on wines and spirits

Qualification: One ordinary or preference share, or any amount of debenture or loan stock, or membership of the Share Ownership Scheme.

Summary of concessions: Shareholders receive with the annual accounts a book containing 16 vouchers with a total value of £45 which can be used towards purchases of at least £300. The book contains two vouchers of £4.50, each of which can be used against goods of at least £30; ten vouchers of £3, each of which can be used against goods of at least £20; and four vouchers of £1.50, each of which can be used against goods of at least £10.

The vouchers may be used to pay for restaurant meals and accommodation at Beefeater Restaurants, Country Club Hotels and Coaching Inns; for restaurant sales at Coaching Inns and Pizza Hut; and to buy wines, beers and minerals at Thresher off-licences.

The vouchers may only be used by the shareholder himself and cannot be used in conjunction with any other special offer vouchers, promotional scheme or discount, or with Whitbread discount vouchers.

Share information at 30 September 1987 ('A' shares):
  Nominal value: 25p
  Price: 324p
  Minimum commitment: £3.24
  Yield: 3.4
  Year's high/low: 579/463p

Yale and Valor plc*

Wood Lane, Erdington, Birmingham B24 9QP. 021-373 8111

Discount on selected products

Qualification: One share

77

Summary of concessions: The company, known as Valor until 23 July 1987, has no set policy regarding shareholder concessions. However, in practice, it usually offers shareholders a discount on selected products.

No offer was made in 1987 but the company has not ruled out offers for future years. In 1986 an offer was made on food processors; in 1985 an offer was made on electric overblankets. These offers were equivalent to a discount of about 25 per cent on the typical high street shop price.

Share information at 30 September 1987:
Nominal value: 25p
Price: 370p
Minimum commitment: £3.70
Yield: 2.1
Year's high/low: 422/278p

Young & Co's Brewery plc*

The Ram Brewery, Wandsworth, London SW18 4JD.   01-870 0141

Free lunch

Qualification: One share, attending the AGM

Summary of concessions: All shareholders who attend the AGM are given a free buffet lunch with wine.

Share information at 30 September 1987 ('A' shares):
Nominal value: 50p
Price: 462p
Minimum commitment: £4.62
Yield: 2.5
Year's high/low: 477/274p

Share information at 30 September 1987 (non-voting):
Nominal value: 50p
Price: 437p
Minimum commitment: £4.37
Yield: 2.7
Year's high/low: 445/235p

Appendices

Appendix 1

Trade Names

As well as offering concessions on products bearing their own name, the listed companies offer concessions under these names:

Alpine Double Glazing (Hawley Group)
Ambrose Wilson (N Brown Group)
Anchor Hotels (Trusthouse Forte)
Angel Hotel (Norfolk Capital Group)
Asteys restaurants (Ladbroke Group)
Athena Bookshops (Pentos)
Athena Galleries (Pentos)
Athenaeum Hotels, London (Rank Organisation)
Austin Rover (Rover Group)
Autolease (BSG International)
George Ballantine (Allied-Lyons)
Barnaby's Carveries (Grand Metropolitan Hotels)
Barratts shops (Stylo)
Beefeater Restaurants (Whitbread)
James Bell & Co (Vaux Group)
Berni Inns (Grand Metropolitan Hotels)
Billersley Hotel (Norfolk Capital Group)
Blue Line Cruisers (Rank Organisation)
Brentfords (Lonrho)
Brigands House Hotel (Norfolk Capital Group)
Bristol Street Motors (BSG International)
Britax seat belts (BSG International)
Browns of Chester shops (Burton Group)
Butlin's holidays (Rank Organisation)
Caledonian Hotel, Edinburgh (Norfolk Capital Group)
Champion Sport shops (Burton Group)

Charbonnel et Walker chocolates (Barker and Dobson Group)
Chef and Brewer (Grand Metropolitan Hotels)
Childrens World (Boots Company)
Club In, Eilat (Ladbroke Group)
Coaching Inns (Whitbread)
Collier shops (Burton Group)
Comfortably Yours (N Brown Group)
Countess Fiona (Allied-Lyons)
Country Club Hotels (Whitbread)
Country Garden (N Brown Group)
Country Gentlemen's Association (Fredericks Place Holdings)
Country Kitchen (N Brown Group)
Crest Hotels (Bass)
Cunard holidays (Trafalgar House)
De Vere hotels (Greenall Whitley)
Debenhams stores (Burton Group)
Derby Tableware (Crown House)
Dillons Bookshop (Pentos)
Dolphin Showers (Hawley Group)
Dutton-Forshaw (Lonrho)
Eastwell Manor Hotel (Norfolk Capital Group)
Edinburgh Crystal (Crown House)
Elms Hotel (Norfolk Capital Group)
Embassy Hotels (Allied-Lyons)
Louis Eschenauer (Lonrho)
Evans shops (Burton Group)
Ewbanks Discount Warehouse (Cattle's (Holdings))
Ewbanks Mail Order (Cattle's (Holdings))
Gieves and Hawkes (Gieves Group)
Gloucester Hotel, London (Rank Organisation)
Goldsmiths (Oriflame International)
Hamleys shops (Burton Group)
Harvey Nichols shops (Burton Group)
Haven Holidays (Rank Organisation)
Heather Valley (N Brown Group)
Hodges Figgis bookshop (Pentos)
Hooks Books (Pentos)
Hospitality Inns (Mount Charlotte Investments)

APPENDIX 1

Hudsons Bookshops (Pentos)
Hudsons Wessex Bookshop (Pentos)
Jackson shops (Burton Group)
Kings Mead hotels (Mount Charlotte Investments)
Kitchens Direct (Hawley Group)
R J Lakin (Berry Birch and Noble)
Land Rover (Rover Group)
Lillywhites (Trusthouse Forte)
Little Chef Restaurants (Trusthouse Forte)
London Park Hotels (Mount Charlotte Investments)
Los Zocos, Lanzarote (Ladbroke Group)
Lygon Arms (Savoy Hotel)
McKenna & Brown (Upton)
McNeill & Co (Manders)
MAN Commercial Vehicles (Lonrho)
Metropole Hotels (Lonrho)
MGB Tiles (Manders)
Mobens Kitchens (Hawley Group)
Money Observer magazine (Lonrho)
New Horizons (N Brown Group)
Nixons kitchen units (Bellway)
North British Hotel, Edinburgh (Norfolk Capital Group)
OSL Travel Plus Club (Rank Organisation)
Oswalds Hotels (Barr and Wallace Arnold Trust)
Oxendale (N Brown Group)
Page and Moy (LWT (Holdings))
Parkhill Travel (Cattle's (Holdings))
Dorothy Perkins shops (Burton Group)
Pizza Hut (Whitbread)
Pontin's holidays (Bass)
Princess Hotels (Lonrho)
Principles shops (Burton Group)
Principles for Men shops (Burton Group)
Rayne UK (Burton Group)
Ring & Brymer (Trusthouse Forte)
Peter Robinson shops (Burton Group)
Rosebys curtains and textiles (Cattle's (Holdings))
Royal Clarence Hotel, Exeter (Norfolk Capital Group)
Royal Court Hotel, London (Norfolk Capital Group)
Royal Crescent Hotel, Bath (Norfolk Capital Group)

Royal Garden Hotel, London (Rank Organisation)
Royal Lancaster Hotel, London (Rank Organisation)
SEAT Concessionaires (Lonrho)
SHARDIS (Rover Group)
Sagafjord World Cruise (Trafalgar House)
St Pierre Park Hotel, Guernsey (Ann Street Breweries)
Sandfords DIY centres (Sharpe & Fisher)
Sharps Bedroom Design (Hawley Group)
Skean Dhu hotels (Mount Charlotte Investments)
Southern Watch and Clock Supplies (Lonrho)
Stop 'n' Steer (Kwik-Fit)
Swallow Hotels (Vaux Group)
Texas Homecare (Ladbroke Group)
Thistle Hotels (Scottish and Newcastle Breweries)
Thresher off-licences (Whitbread)
Top Man shops (Burton Group)
Top Shop (Burton Group)
Townsend Thorensen (European Ferries Group)
Travelplan (Cattle's (Holdings))
Trust Motors (Barr and Wallace Arnold Trust)
Turners Furnishing (Cattle's) (Holdings))
UBM building supplies (Norcros)
Unicorn Hotel, Bristol (Rank Organsiation)
VAG (Lonrho)
Valor (Yale and Valor)
Victoria Wine Stores (Allied-Lyons)
Wallace Arnold Tours (Barr and Wallace Arnold Trust)
S H Ward (Vaux Group)
WASS (Barr and Wallace Arnold Trust)
Weatherheads Bookshop (Pentos)
Weatherseal Double Glazing (Evered Holdings)
Thomas Webb Crystal (Crown House)
Whyte and Mackay (Lonrho)
J D Williams (N Brown Group)
Wine Growers Association (Trusthouse Forte)

Appendix 2

Index of Concessions Offered

Antiques:	Asprey
Books:	David & Charles
	Pentos
Business planner:	Allied-Lyons
Car leasing:	BSG International
Car servicing:	Barr and Wallace Arnold Trust
	BSG International
	Kwik-Fit
Cars:	Alexanders Holdings
	BSG International
	Lonrho
	Rover Group
Clocks and watches:	*see jewellery*
Clothes:	Alexon Group
	Burton Group
	Gieves Group
	John Kent (Menswear)
	Moss Bros
Clothes hire:	Moss Bros
Club membership:	Fredericks Place Holdings
Confectionery:	Barker and Dobson Group
	Alfred Preedy
Contact lenses:	Grand Metropolitan Hotels
Credit facilities:	Burton Group (card)
	Cattle's (Holdings) (Shopachecks)

PERKS FROM SHARES

Cruises:	Allied-Lyons
	Barclays Unicorn Unit Trusts
	Trafalgar House
Domestic goods:	Bentalls
	Boots Company
	Cattle's (Holdings)
	Courts (furniture)
	Crown House (tableware)
	Emess Lighting (light fittings)
	Fobel International
	Kalon Group (paint and wallpaper)
	Ladbroke Group
	Lonrho (bedding and soft furnishings)
	Manders (paint, brushes, wall coverings)
	Mellerware International (cookware and small items)
	Norcros (building and DIY materials)
	Alfred Preedy
	Upton
	Yale and Valor
Double glazing:	Hawley Group
Draw:	Dominion International
	Manchester and London Investment Trust
Drink:	Allied-Lyons
	Fredericks Place Holdings
	Fuller Smith & Turner
	Grand Metropolitan Hotels
	Greene King
	Lonrho
	Merrydown Wine
	Scottish and Newcastle Breweries
	Trusthouse Forte
	Whitbread & Company
Dry cleaning:	Sketchley
Ferries:	DFDS
	European Ferries Group

APPENDIX 2

	Isle of Man Steam Packet Seaways
	Peninsular and Oriental Steam Navigation
	Southampton Isle of Wight and South of England Royal Mail Steam Packet
Fine arts:	Asprey
	Pentos
Food:	Associated British Foods
	Hillards
	Park Food Group
	Ranks Hovis McDougall
Furniture:	*see domestic goods*
Garden equipment:	Cramphorn
	Sharpe & Fisher
Gift at AGM:	Beecham Group
	Guinness
	Pacific Sales Organisation
	Ranks Hovis McDougall
Greyhound racing:	GRA Group
Holidays:	Barr and Wallace Arnold Trust
	Bass
	Cattle's (Holdings)
	Dominion International Group (free draw for)
	Ladbroke Group
	LWT (Holdings)
	Rank Organisation
	Stakis
	Trafalgar House
Home improvements:	Hawley Group
	Sharpe & Fisher (DIY materials)
Hotels:	Allied-Lyons
	Ann Street Brewery
	Barr and Wallace Arnold Trust
	Bass
	Greenall Whitley
	Ladbroke Group
	Lonrho
	Mount Charlotte Investments

PERKS FROM SHARES

	Norfolk Capital Group
	Rank Organisation
	Savoy Hotel
	Scottish and Newcastle Breweries
	Stakis
	Trafalgar House
	Trusthouse Forte
	Vaux Group
	Whitbread & Company
Houses:	Barratt Developments
	Bellway
Insurance:	Berry Birch and Noble
Jewellery:	Asprey
	Lonrho
	Oriflame International
	Toye & Company (also regalia, trophies, badges etc)
Kitchen units:	Bellway
	Hawley Group
Lunch at AGM:	Cliffords Dairies
	Eldridge Pope
	Vaux Group
	Young & Co
Magazines:	Fredericks Place Holdings (*Your Money*)
	Lonrho (*Money Observer*)
Mail order:	N Brown Group
	Cattle's (Holdings)
Meals:	Allied-Lyons
	Garfunkels Restaurants
	Grand Metropolitan Hotels
	Kennedy Brookes
	Ladbroke Group
	Queens Moat Houses
	Scottish and Newcastle Breweries
	Stakis
	Trusthouse Forte
	Vaux Group
Pets' items:	Cramphorn

APPENDIX 2

Pharamaceutical products:	Beecham Group
	Boots Company
Railway journey:	North Norfolk Railway plc
	Romney Hythe & Dymchurch Railway
	Severn Valley Railway
Security systems:	Britannia Security Group
School fees:	Abercorn Place School
Seat belts:	BSG International
Shoes:	Burton Group
	Stylo
Spectacles:	Grand Metropolitan Hotels
Sportswear:	Burton Group
	Grand Metropolitan Hotels
	Stylo
	Trusthouse Forte
Tennis matches:	All England Lawn Tennis Ground
Timeshare:	Trafalgar House
Toys:	Boots Company
Unit trusts:	Abbey Life
	Britannia-Arrow Holdings
Visit to castle:	Ferguson

Appendix 3

Rating of Concessions Offered

This appendix gives a necessarily subjective rating on the value of the concessions offered.

*** Three stars mean that the concession will normally be a factor in deciding whether to hold shares in the company.

** Two stars mean that the concession may be valuable enough to swing a marginal decision in favour of investing in that company.

* One star denotes that the concession is unlikely to influence a decision to buy that share, though the concession may still be worth having.

*** Concessions likely to influence the decision whether to buy the share

　　Abercorn Place School plc
　　All England Lawn Tennis Ground
　　Barratt Developments plc
　　Bellway plc
　　European Ferries Group plc
　　North Norfolk Railway plc
　　Romney Hythe & Dymchurch Railway plc
　　Severn Valley Railway (Holdings) plc
　　Southampton Isle of Wight and South of England Royal
　　　　Mail Steam Packet plc

** **Could influence the decision whether to buy the share**
  Abbey Life Assurance Company Ltd
  Alexanders Holdings plc
  Alexon Group plc
  Asprey plc
  Barclays Unicorn Unit Trusts
  Bass plc
  Britannia-Arrow Holdings
  BSG International plc
  Burton Group plc
  DFDS (UK) Ltd
  Fobel International plc
  Hawley Group plc
  Hillards plc
  Kalon Group plc
  Ladbroke Group plc
  Lonrho plc
  Manders (Holdings) plc
  Merrydown Wine plc
  Norfolk Capital Group plc
  Alfred Preedy plc
  Rover Group plc
  Sketchley plc
  Stakis plc
  Stylo plc
  Trusthouse Forte plc

* **Unlikely to influence a decision whether to buy a share, though probably worth having**
  Allied-Lyons plc
  Ann Street Brewery plc
  Associated British Foods plc
  Barker and Dobson Group
  Barr and Wallace Arnold Trust plc
  Beecham Group plc
  Bentalls plc
  Berry Birch and Noble plc
  Boots Company plc
  Britannia Security Group plc
  N Brown Group plc

Cattle's (Holdings) plc
Cliffords Dairies plc
Courts (Furnishers) plc
Cramphorn plc
Crown House plc
David & Charles Publishers plc
Dominion International Group plc
Eldridge Pope & Co Ltd
Emess Lighting plc
Evered Holdings plc
Ferguson Industrial Holdings plc
Fredericks Place Holdings plc
Fuller Smith & Turner plc
Garfunkels Restaurants plc
Gieves Group plc
GRA Group plc
Grand Metropolitan Hotels plc
Greenall Whitley plc
Greene King and Sons plc
Guinness plc
Isle of Man Steam Packet Seaways
Kennedy Brookes plc
John Kent (Menswear) Ltd
Kwik-Fit (Tyres & Exhausts) Holdings plc
LWT (Holdings) plc
Manchester and London Investment Trust
Mellerware International plc
Moss Bros
Mount Charlotte Investments plc
Norcros plc
Oriflame International SA
Pacific Sales Organisation
Park Food Group plc
Peninsular and Oriental Steam Navigation Company
Pentos plc
Queens Moat Houses plc
Rank Organisation plc
Ranks Hovis McDougall plc
Savoy Hotel plc
Scottish and Newcastle Breweries plc

Sharpe & Fisher plc
Toye & Company plc
Trafalgar House plc iE Upton & Sons plc
E Upton & Sons plc
Vaux Group plc
Whitbread & Company plc
Yale and Valor plc
Young & Co's Brewery plc

Appendix 4

Value of Minimum Consideration

The list below gives the minimum amount you would have had to invest in shares at their 30 September 1987 values to obtain the concessions offered to shareholders:

£15,960	Southampton Isle of Wight and South of England Royal Mail Steam Packet
£10,642.50	Asprey
£4320	Merrydown Wine
£3520	Rank Organisation
£3046.88	Moss Bros
£2880	Bellway
£2320	Kennedy Brookes
£2250	Barratt Developments
£2115	Britannia-Arrow Holdings
£1555	Mount Charlotte Investments
£1518	Gieves Group
£1491	Sketchley
£1476	Peninsular and Oriental Steam Navigation (deferred)
£1355	Trusthouse Forte
£1008	LWT (Holdings)
£995	Trafalgar House
£885	Pentos
£870	Alexanders Holdings
£864	Burton Group

PERKS FROM SHARES

£790	Hawley Group
£762.50	Oriflame International
£760	Berry Birch and Noble
£730	Barr and Wallace Arnold Trust
£700	Peninsular and Oriental Steam Navigation (preferred)
£605	John Kent (Menswear)
£600	Dominion International Group
£575	Toye & Company
£501	Emess Lighting
£500	Rover Group
£433	Alexon Group
£422.50	Alfred Preedy
£387.50	E Upton & Sons
£366	Stakis
£334.50	Lonrho
£306	Boots Company
£282.50	Mellerware International
£270	Courts (Furnishers)
£220	Kwik-Fit (Tyres and Exhausts) Holdings
£178	Bentalls
£10	Bass
£8.90	N Brown
£6.58	Savoy Hotel
£5.81	Beecham Group
£5.79	Grand Metropolitan Hotels
£5.69	Vaux Group
£5.56	Cliffords Dairies
£5.35	Fuller Smith & Turner
£4.53	Ladbroke Group
£4.42	Allied-Lyons
£4.37	Young & Co
£4.33	Norcros
£4.31	Greene King
£3.93	Eldridge Pope & Co
£3.92	Ferguson Industrial Holdings
£3.85	Manders (Holdings)
£3.75	Pacific Sales Organisation
£3.72	Guinness
£3.70	Yale and Valor

APPENDIX 4

£3.57	Ranks Hovis McDougall
£3.43	Associated British Foods
£3.36	Stylo
£3.35½	Abbey Life Assurance Company
£3.24	Whitbread & Company
£3.23	Evered Holdings
£2.93	Park Food Group
£2.61	Scottish and Newcastle Breweries
£2.60	Garfunkels Restaurants
£2.46	Greenall Whitley
£2.44	Britannia Security Group
£2.43	Sharpe & Fisher
£2.26	Barker and Dobson
£1.72	Fobel International
£1.50	GRA Group
£1.09	Queens Moat Houses
96¾p	BSG International
47½p	Kalon Group
41½p	Norfolk Capital Group

Other Books by Blackstone Franks

Property Tax Tolley's 17 Scarbrook Rd Croydon Surrey CR0 1SQ. The definitive guide to planning points and clear exposition of this most complex area.

The Economist Guide to Management Buy-Outs Economist Publications 40 Duke St London W1A 1DW. The third edition of this book. Blackstone Franks advise on management buy-outs.

Raising Money for Business Economist Publications. A clearly written book to help you prepare your business proposal.

The Economist Guide to Business Expansion Schemes Economist Publications. Edited by Blackstone Franks and includes chapters on tax, law and prospectuses.

Crawford Corporate Finance Economist Publications. Directory of city finance.

The Blackstone Franks Good Investment Guide Kogan Page 120 Pentonville Rd London N1 9JN. An insider guide to the A to Z of investment opportunities, all rated.

The UK as a Tax Haven Economist Publications. Now in its 3rd edition, a layman's guide to tax planning in the UK.

The Blackstone Franks Guide to Living in Spain Kogan Page. Due Spring 1988.

Tolley's Tax Planning Tolley's. Contributed chapters on emigration and passing down the family business.

Tax Case Analysis Oyez Longman 21-27 Lamb's Conduit St London WC1. Blackstone Franks are consulting editors.

Anti Avoidance Legislation Tolley's. A comprehensive review of all legislation aimed at preventing the avoidance of tax.

PERKS FROM SHARES

Taxation of Non-Resident Entertainers & Sportsmen
Tolley's. A detailed report setting out the exact effect of taxation on entertainers and sportsmen.
Tax Minimisation Techniques Oyez Longman. 4th edition of this report on the methods of minimising taxation.
Fringe Benefits Oyez Longman. 3rd edition covering taxation of fringe benefits.

Blackstone Franks & Co
Chartered Accountants & Investment Managers
26-34 Old Street
London EC1V 9HL

Personal Finance Titles from Kogan Page

Easing into Retirement, Keith Hughes, 1987
How to Invest Successfully, 2nd edn, Felicity Taylor, 1986
Inheritance Tax: A Practical Guide, 2nd edn, Barry Stillerman, 1988
Living and Retiring Abroad, 2nd edn, Michael Furnell, 1988
Personal Pensions: The Choice is Yours, Norman Toulson, 1987

Index

Abbey Life Assurance Company Ltd 19, 89, 92, 96
Abercorn Place School plc 19, 89, 91
Alexanders Holdings plc 20, 85, 92, 95
Alexon group plc 21, 85, 92, 96
All England Lawn Tennis Ground 21, 89, 91
Allied-Lyons plc 22, 81, 82, 84, 85, 86, 87, 88, 92, 96
Ann Street Brewery plc 23, 84, 87, 92
Asprey plc 23, 85, 87, 88, 92, 95
Associated British Foods plc 24, 87, 92, 96
Barclays Unicorn Trusts 24, 86, 92
Barker & Dobson Group 25, 82, 85, 92, 96
Barr and Wallace Arnold Trust plc 25, 83, 84, 85, 87, 92, 96
Barratt Developments plc 26, 88, 91, 95
Bass plc 7, 27, 82, 83, 87, 92, 96
Beecham Group plc 7, 8, 28, 87, 89, 92, 96
Bellway plc 28, 83, 88, 91, 95
Bentalls plc 2, 29, 86, 92, 96
Berry Birch and Noble plc 29, 83, 88, 92, 96
Boots Company plc 30, 82, 86, 89, 92, 96
BP 11, 12
Britannia-Arrow Holdings 30, 89, 92, 95
Britannia Security Group plc 31, 89, 92, 96
British Gas 11, 13, 14
British Telecom 11, 13, 14
Britoil 12
N Brown Group plc 31, 81, 83, 84, 88, 92, 96
BSG International plc 32, 81, 85, 89, 92, 96
Burton group plc 8, 33, 81, 82, 83, 84, 85, 89, 92, 95
Cattle's (Holdings) plc 34, 82, 83, 84, 85, 86, 87, 88, 93
Cliffords Dairies plc 8, 35, 88, 93, 96
Courts (Furnishers) plc 35, 86, 93, 96
Cramphorn plc 36, 87, 88, 93
Crown House plc 36, 82, 84, 86, 93
David & Charles Publishers plc 37, 85, 93

DFDS (UK) Ltd 37, 86, 92
Dominion International Group plc 38, 86, 87, 93, 96
Eldridge Pope & Co Ltd 38, 88, 93, 96
Emess Lighting plc 39, 86, 93, 96
European Ferries group plc 8, 39, 84, 86, 91
Evered Holdings plc 7, 41, 84, 93, 96
Ferguson Industrial Holdings plc 42, 89, 93, 96
Fobel International plc 8, 42, 86, 92, 96
Fredericks Place Holdings plc 43, 82, 85, 86, 88, 93
Fuller Smith & Turner plc 43, 86, 93, 96
Garfunkels Restaurants plc 44, 88, 93, 96
Gieves Group plc 44, 82, 85, 93, 95
GRA Group plc 45, 87, 93, 96
Grand Metropolitan Hotels plc 45, 81, 82, 85, 86, 88, 89, 93, 96
Greenall Whitley plc 46, 82, 87, 93, 96
Greene King and Sons plc 47, 86, 93, 96
Guinness plc 8, 47, 87, 93, 96
Hawley Group plc 48, 81, 82, 83, 84, 86, 87, 88, 92, 96
Hillards plc 48, 87, 92
Isle of Man Steam Packet Seaways 49, 87, 93
Kalon Group plc 49, 86, 92, 96
Kennedy Brookes plc 50, 88, 93, 95
John Kent (Menswear) Ltd 50, 85, 93, 96
Kwik-Fit (Tyres & Exhausts) Holdings plc 51, 84, 85, 93, 96
Ladbroke Group plc 51, 81, 82, 83, 84, 86, 87, 88, 92, 96
Lonrho plc 9, 53, 81, 82, 83, 84, 85, 86, 87, 88, 92, 96
LWT (Holdings) plc 55, 83, 87, 93, 95
Manchester and London Investment Trust 55, 86, 93
Manders (Holdings) plc 56, 83, 86, 92, 96
Mellerware international plc 9, 56, 86, 93, 96
Merrydown Wine plc 57, 86, 92, 95
Moss Bros 57, 85, 93, 95
Mount Charlotte Investments plc 58, 82, 83, 84, 87, 93, 95
Norcros plc 58, 84, 93, 96
Norfolk Capital Group plc 59, 81, 82, 83, 84, 88, 92, 96
North Norfolk Railway plc 60, 89, 91
Oriflame International SA 60, 82, 88, 93, 96
Pacific Sales Organisation 61, 87, 93, 96
Park Food Group plc 62, 87, 93, 96

INDEX

Peninsular and Orient Steam Navigation Company 8, 62, 87, 93, 95, 96
Pentos plc 63, 81, 82, 83, 84, 85, 87, 93, 95
Alfred Preedy plc 64, 85, 86, 92, 96
Queens Moat Houses plc 64, 88, 93, 96
Rank Organisation plc 7, 65, 81, 82, 83, 84, 87, 88, 93, 95
Ranks Hovis McDougall plc 66, 87, 93, 96
Romney Hythe & Dymchurch Railway plc 66, 89, 91
Rover Group plc 67, 81, 83, 84, 85, 92, 96
Savoy Hotel plc 68, 83, 88, 93, 96
Scottish and Newcastle Breweries plc 68, 84, 86, 88, 93, 96
Severn Valley Railway (Holdings) plc 69, 89, 91
Sharpe & Fisher plc 69, 84, 87, 94, 96
Sketchley plc 9, 70, 86, 92, 95
Southampton Isle of Wight and South of England Royal Mail Steam Packet plc 71, 87, 91, 95
Stakis plc 72, 87, 88, 92, 96
Stylo plc 72, 81, 89, 92, 96
Thorn-EMI 7
Toye & Company plc 73, 88, 94, 96
Trafalgar House plc 73, 82, 84, 86, 87, 88, 89, 94, 95
Trustee Savings Bank 11
Trusthouse Forte plc 9, 74, 81, 83, 84, 86, 88, 89, 92, 95
E Upton & Sons plc 75, 83, 86, 94, 96
Vaux Group plc 76, 81, 84, 88, 94, 96
Whitbread & Company plc 77, 81, 82, 83, 84, 86, 88, 94, 96
Williams Holdings 7
Yale & Valor plc 77, 84, 86, 94, 96
Young & Co's Brewery plc 78, 88, 94, 96